Critical Guides to French Texts

7 Balzac: Illusions perdues

Critical Guides to French Texts

EDITED BY ROGER LITTLE, WOLFGANG VAN EMDEN,
DAVID WILLIAMS

BALZAC

Illusions perdues

Donald Adamson

Principal Lecturer in French
Goldsmiths' College, London

Grant & Cutler Ltd
1981

I.S.B.N. 84-499-4784-7

DEPÓSITO LEGAL: V. 1.590 - 1981

Printed in Spain by
Artes Gráficas Soler, S. A. - Olivereta, 18 - Valencia (18)
for

GRANT & CUTLER LTD
11 BUCKINGHAM STREET, LONDON, W.C.2.

Contents

Preface

Tʜɪs is a book for both sixth-formers and university and college students. I hope that it will prove useful not only to those readers for whom *Illusions perdues* is a prescribed text but also to students of Balzac generally.

Its main emphasis is upon the middle section of the novel, *Un Grand Homme de province à Paris*. Even so, the attempt is made to present *Illusions perdues* as a rounded whole. Those who wish for fuller knowledge of the character of Lucien de Rubempré should, however, go on to read *Splendeurs et misères des courtisanes*. For a proper understanding of Vautrin alias Carlos Herrera, a reading of *Le Père Goriot* is also helpful.

Not all the aspects of such a complex novel as *Illusions perdues* can be considered in a work of this length. I have analysed in some detail those aspects which seem to me to be fundamental. It is for the student, using this Critical Guide as a working instrument, to examine other features of the text for himself.

All quotations from *Illusions perdues* are from the Garnier Flammarion edition of the novel. References to the works listed in the Bibliography give the number of the edition, book or article in italics, followed by the page number(s), e.g. (*35*, p. 53). References to *Illusions perdues* itself merely give, within brackets, the page number(s) of the Garnier Flammarion edition.

D.A.

1

Introduction

ILLUSIONS perdues, one of the longest of the ninety-four novels which make up the *Comédie humaine*, is also perhaps the one which best illustrates Balzac's distinctive approach to the novel form. Almost all the major themes which preoccupy him as a writer are contained within it; and, broadly speaking, they are treated with exceptional skill. In the first and second parts of the novel, if not in the whole work, he is writing at the very height of his powers. It is indeed arguable that Part II, *Un Grand Homme de province à Paris*, is the finest thing he ever wrote. 'L'œuvre capitale dans l'œuvre' (*4* (2), p. 172) was his own description of the full-length *Illusions perdues*.

A first major preoccupation of Balzac in *Illusions perdues* is that of the interrelationship of Paris and the provinces. Part I of the novel, *Les Deux Poètes*, is set in Angoulême and ends with the departure of Lucien de Rubempré, one of the two poets (and one of the two heroes), for Paris. Paris becomes the setting of the second, and by far the longest, part of the novel. *Les Souffrances de l'inventeur*, the third and last part of *Illusions perdues*, bestrides Paris and the provinces: though it is essentially set in Angoulême, the repercussions of Paris upon the provinces (and, in particular, those of Lucien's conduct in Paris upon the lives of his sister and brother-in-law) are constantly evident.

A second theme of profound importance both in the *Comédie humaine* as a whole and here in *Illusions perdues* is that of the artist: his struggles with intractable inspiration, his temptations to slip into an easy path rather than to choose the path of strenuous endeavour; and the nature of his artistic achievement. Lucien and David Séchard are, in Balzac's eyes, both artists. Lucien is the author of a sonnet-sequence and a historical novel. David is a scientist the summit of whose achievement is to invent a cheaper method of paper manufacture. Nevertheless, despite the apparent differences in their callings, they are *les deux poètes* since both are in a sense inventors; each hopes to *find* the fulfilment of the inspiration working within him, and to make some new discovery whether in the arts or the sciences. Balzac believes in the fraternity of all those — poets, novelists, chemists, philosophers and even men of action — who seek through the exercise both of imagination and of will-power to create new worlds. From this point of view it is important, symbolically, that Lucien and David become brothers-in-law. Even before David's marriage to Ève (which occurs just after the end of Part I) Balzac is at pains to stress the brotherly relationship of these two young artists in the making.

A third aspect of *Illusions perdues* is that of the *Bildungsroman*: the novel, after the pattern of Goethe's *Wilhelm Meisters Lehrjahre* or Balzac's own *Le Père Goriot,* tracing the development and growing maturity of a young man in his contacts with the world. *Le Père Goriot,* published about two years before *Illusions perdues* was begun, had described the *Bildung,* or formative experiences, of a young man (Eugène de Rastignac) rapidly learning how to conduct himself and to achieve social success in Paris. In *Illusions perdues* Balzac now describes the opposite process, whereby Lucien — exposed to all the pitfalls and temptations of the capital — makes many mistakes, fails to learn from them, and instead of achieving the success achieved by Rastignac suffers humiliation, confusion and disgrace.

Fourthly, we see in *Illusions perdues* (more clearly, perhaps, than in any other novel of the *Comédie humaine*) evidence of Balzac's wish to present a comprehensive picture of society. A year before the completion of Part III of *Illusions perdues,* Balzac had explained in his *Avant-propos* to the first collective edition of his novels that a major aim of his was to write the social history of France in the first half of the nineteenth century (*I*(1), p. 11). And in this purpose, especially after the completion of *Illusions perdues,* he gradually came to feel that he had succeeded. He is concerned with historical truth in the broadest sense, wishing to convey the atmosphere of the society in which he lived, and to create a faithful and sensitive impression of the forces that were at work within that society. Only by elevating the individual characters of his novel — and, in particular, David Séchard, Daniel d'Arthez, Étienne Lousteau, Vautrin and (in some sense) Lucien and Coralie — to the status of types, only by extracting the general truth from the particular instance, can Balzac achieve that historical purpose so often stressed in the novel. The particular circumstances of the nineteenth century present those who live in that era, and especially its youth, with special problems and difficulties. Balzac must not 'représenter le jeune homme autrement qu'il n'est au dix-neuvième siècle' (88). At the Terrasse des Feuillants in the Tuileries gardens Lucien 'rencontra plusieurs de ces femmes dont on parlera dans l'histoire du dix-neuvième siècle' (183). 'Si tes sonnets', Dauriat tells Lucien at their first meeting, 'sont à la hauteur du dix-neuvième siècle, je ferai de toi... un grand poète' (276). Balzac even describes the young men and women of the nineteenth century, especially the young men, as living in the colossal shadow of Napoleon, 'si fatal au dix-neuvième siècle par les prétentions qu'il inspire à tant de gens médiocres' (90). Yet if, in a very real sense, Balzac is the historian of nineteenth-century France in *Illusions perdues,* he is also — according to the terms of Herrera's distinction (590) — its secret, rather than its official, historian.

A final feature of *Illusions perdues* shared with other works by Balzac is the presence within it of many recurring characters. These are characters who occur from novel to novel within the *Comédie humaine,* sometimes — like Rastignac, who makes twenty-four appearances — recurring in many novels and short stories, occasionally at the centre of a particular plot but more usually in varying degrees of secondary importance. *Illusions perdues* and its sequel *Splendeurs et misères des courtisanes* are an immense meeting-place of the leading characters of the *Comédie humaine,* from which paths radiate outwards into the most unfrequented corners of Balzac's imaginary universe. Lucien, moreover, is the only one of Balzac's heroes to be given full-scale treatment in two novels. In all other instances of recurring characters, a character who is the actual hero of one

novel will not be the hero of another. Rastignac, who receives
his fullest treatment as the *young* hero of *Le Père Goriot*, is
of merely episodic importance in *Illusions perdues*. Daniel
d'Arthez, an important but by no means the principal character
of *Un Grand Homme de province à Paris*, will later become the
hero of *Les Secrets de la Princesse de Cadignan*.

Linked to Lucien's exceptional status as the hero of two
novels is the fact that the Abbé Carlos Herrera becomes his
mentor towards the end of *Illusions perdues* and continues to
be so throughout *Splendeurs et misères des courtisanes*. Herrera's sudden and at first surprising appearance just in time to
rescue Lucien from suicide is his first reappearance in the
Comédie humaine, his original presentation being (as Rastignac's mentor, Vautrin) in *Le Père Goriot*. Thus, it can be said
that *Le Père Goriot, Illusions perdues* and *Splendeurs et misères des courtisanes* form a kind of Vautrin cycle in which
Vautrin — though never the principal figure of any of the three
novels [1] — himself undergoes a *Bildung* or evolution.

The presence of such recurring characters in *Illusions perdues* is itself evidence of the novel's professedly historical nature. For in a recognizably authentic world — whether the world
of 'real' history or that of 'imaginary' fiction — all the parts that
compose it cannot be totally distinct from one another. An
event which occurred in one novel will be mentioned, either in
the authorial discourse or in the characters' dialogue, in some
other work. Key figures will be present in several or many of
the novels and short stories. The palpable impression of a historical reality is imparted to *Illusions perdues* no less by the
references to the Cénacle (225-230), the Rastignacs (108), Ca-
mille Maupin (444, 446), the *Huile céphalique* (252) and Gi-
roudeau (239) than by those to Napoleon, Villèle (387), the
Didots (42, 43, 47) and Martainville (417, 419). *Illusions perdues*
creates a fictional alternative to the actual historical world, a
territory in which individuals are raised to the stature of types
and where these typical beings embody some of the characteristics of myth.

---

[1] Herrera/Vautrin makes a further, very brief appearance in *La
Cousine Bette* (*1*(7), p. 402), and is the hero of one of Balzac's plays.

2

The Polarization of the Two Heroes

W HEN Lucien is first presented to the reader, it is in company with the second and alternative hero of *Illusions perdues,* David Séchard (54-61). At first sight, the two young men appear to be polar opposites: David is solidly built, dark and masculine; Lucien is slim, fair and feminine. Within this system of polar opposites there are, however, many resemblances: David is shown to have literary leanings (61); Lucien is scientifically inclined (56). Lucien's father was also a scientist. It was, in fact, M. Chardon who first conceived the idea of using vegetable fibres in a new method of paper manufacture (57, 133), an idea which during the remainder of the novel David Séchard will struggle to implement. A further point of resemblance between two young men who to outward appearances are so different is the deep friendship arising from such an affinity of tastes and interests. Repeatedly (63, 97, 125) they refer to each other as brothers, even before (just after the close of *Les Deux Poètes*: at the intersection, as it were, of Parts I and II) they become brothers-in-law. Theirs is a spiritual relationship long before it becomes a legal one.

This intermingling of similarities within a system of apparent contradictions reflects what is true on a wider scale throughout *Illusions perdues*: that distinctions — whether between the Royalist and Liberal parties, or between the Royalist and Liberal newspapers, or between Petit-Claud and the Cointets, or even between the Cénacle and journalism — are not as clearcut as they may seem. Conversely, within the fraternity of friendship there are hidden antagonisms: in *Un Grand Homme de province à Paris,* within the fellowship of Lucien and the Cénacle; and, throughout *Illusions perdues,* within the fellowship of Lucien and David. Between the young 'poets' two points of clear distinction can be noted. They concern family loyalty and the seeking of secrets.

David is strong in his loyalty both to his family and to the wider social unit. 'Je voudrais être le frère de Lucien', he exclaims (125): this wish is presented as one of his reasons for wishing to marry Ève Chardon, his affection for Lucien uniting him with Ève's love for her brother. David welcomes Ève's mother into the family (134); he builds an extra storey on to his house as a home for Lucien (134, 137, 142-143). In his attitude towards society generally he has a remarkably clear sense of his own personal identity, of his comparative unimportance as an individual within the wider community, and of the duty incumbent on every citizen to promote the well-being of the society of which he is a member. As early as Part I, and before his marriage, he says to his friend:

> Ma vie, à moi, Lucien, est arrêtée. Je suis David Séchard, imprimeur du roi à Angoulême, et dont le nom se lit sur tous les murs au bas des affiches (96).

Regarding the taking of his great secret by the Cointet brothers, he consoles himself thus:

> Les Cointet profiteront certainement de ma découverte; mais après tout, que suis-je relativement à mon pays?... Un homme. Si mon secret profite à tous, eh! bien, je suis content! (610)

And indeed, in the ultimate historical analysis, David's efforts enrich not only the Cointets themselves but France as a whole (624).

Contrast these statements with Lucien's attitude towards both his own family and society at large. Lucien is ashamed of David:

> Si madame de Bargeton consent à devenir madame de Rubempré, jamais elle ne voudra se trouver être la belle-sœur de David Séchard! (133)
>
> Il avait besoin de faire accepter le mariage de sa sœur à cette femme [Mme de Bargeton] (139).

Lucien is also ashamed of the memory of his dead father, despite the latter's brilliance as a pharmacist and chemist. This shame is manifested in his obsessive desire to change his surname from Chardon to De Rubempré. Such shame is the reflection of personal vanity. As Lucien walks home through the streets of Angoulême, the crestfallen prodigal son rather than the *grand homme de province,* Balzac wryly comments: 'il vit avec plaisir (tant sa vanité conservait de force) le nom de son père effacé' (541).

As for Lucien's attitude towards society as a whole, from first to last he displays profound egoism. Rather than be content (as David is) with fitting into his own niche within society, he is the social climber intent upon making his way regardless of the feelings and wishes of others. Witness, for example, the ruthlessness with which he ignores the invitation to his sister's wedding in order to elope to Paris with Mme de Bargeton (160). At the high points in his fortunes (and there is one occurrence of these in each of the three parts), he is gracefully ambitious but also vain, hectoring and eager to triumph both over his friends and his enemies. At all times he is thoughtless of the consequences of his actions, whether in moments of triumph or of despair.

In their seeking of their respective secrets the two young men are again vividly contrasted. David seeks, and discovers, two secrets: first, a method of manufacturing paper from vegetable fibres (483); and later (530), the method of sizing vegetable pulp in a vat which is necessary for large-scale production. Both his secrets are commercially exploitable. Lucien also discovers two secrets in the sense that, by the power of his imagination, he creates two works of art out of the void. These are his sonnet-sequence *Les Marguerites* and his historical novel *L'Archer de Charles IX.* His work on both is well advanced by the time when *Illusions perdues* opens: he has been busy with the novel for two years (143), and it seems that he has already completed the sonnets; both works are finished by the end of Part I. This contrasts with the fact that the first of David's secrets — the method of using nettles and similar vegetable fibres in paper manufacture — is not even remotely discerned until page 483, and not fully grasped until pages

501-502, of *Les Souffrances de l'inventeur,* whilst the technique
of sizing in a vat is not discovered until towards the very end
(530) of the Angoulême flashback in Part III (460-536). But the
still greater point of contrast between David's and Lucien's
seeking of secrets is that, whereas David's secrets are both commercially valuable, Lucien's are not.

Let us briefly consider the fate of Lucien's two serious literary works. [1] The copyright of the sonnet-sequence is bought by
Dauriat for 3,000 francs (356, 432), but only as an effective
and ultimately inexpensive method of buying off Lucien's hostility as a reviewer: in *Illusions perdues* the sonnets are never
published. The historical novel, after various rejections, is sold
to the speculators Fendant and Cavalier not for hard cash but
for promissory notes to the value of 5,000 francs (404). But
when *L'Archer de Charles IX* is published, it is a complete
failure (439), Fendant and Cavalier go bankrupt, and Lucien
who had negotiated their promissory notes for 4,500 francs with
Camusot (426) now finds himself being sued by Camusot for
the recovery of the debt (440). Lucien's novel is remaindered
and hawked by book-pedlars in the streets and on the bridges
of Paris, and along the Seine embankments. Only later, in 1824
(by which time the action of *Illusions perdues* has effectively
come to an end), [2] does *L'Archer de Charles IX* come into its
own (439). Its second edition, prefaced by Daniel d'Arthez, is
a success, and — as we learn from *Splendeurs et misères des
courtisanes* (*I*(6), p. 488)—the sonnet-sequence, when eventually
published, sells out within a week. Within the main framework
of the action of *Illusions perdues,* however, the fate of Lucien's
poetry and novel confirms the basic situation of the publishing
trade as outlined by Lousteau (250-256). Consequently, Lucien

---

[1] Lucien is also the author of two other poems, both inspired by
the Bible: 'Saint Jean dans Pathmos' and 'Le Festin de Balthazar' (95,
98, 119). But Balzac lays no emphasis on these.

[2] Taken as a whole, *Illusions perdues* covers the period from (early)
May 1821 to 1842. Part I, besides flashbacks to earlier periods such
as David's schooling in Paris, covers the four months from May to
September 1821. Part II extends from September 1821 to October 1822.
The action of Part III stretches, in the main, from September/October
1822 until September 1823. The nineteen subsequent years are lightly
alluded to in the rapid updating of the action on pages 624-625.

would have fared in exactly the same way *as a creative writer* if he had remained at Angoulême.

This prompts the central question: to what extent, notwithstanding the title of Part I (*Les Deux Poètes*), should Lucien be considered a type or archetype of the Poet? If the problem which he faces — that of arousing interest in his creative literary works and of finding himself a publisher — is not so much his personal problem as that of every poet, is his a symbolic destiny? For if indeed, as György Lukács suggests (*35*, p. 53), Lucien should be regarded as an archetype of the Poet, 'le nouveau type de poète spécifiquement bourgeois', then Part II in its descriptions of the young man's misfortunes in Paris is social criticism, in the manner of Vigny's *Chatterton,* castigating an indifferent society for the harsh treatment it metes out to the poet.

Unquestionably, Lousteau's warnings concerning the hardships besetting the serious literary artist in Paris are stamped with the authority and basic authorial impartiality of social criticism. The fact that Lucien's two works achieve renown two years or so after the ending of *Un Grand Homme de province à Paris* in no way detracts from the fundamental accuracy of Lousteau's analysis, for this eventual success is largely a *succès d'estime* due to Lucien's tardily achieved social eminence. This in itself indicates that Lucien's poetic destiny is by no means a representative one. More precisely, his poetic career is a vivid illustration of one sort of fate that can befall the man of poetic leanings. In his letter to Ève Séchard in Part III, D'Arthez specifically denies that Lucien is a poet: 'Votre Lucien est un homme de poésie et non un poète, il rêve et ne pense pas, il s'agite et ne crée pas...' (478). The references to Lucien as a poet in Part I (including the title of the first Part) are, therefore, references to the *potential* rather than the *actual* poet; and this is so even though *Les Marguerites* and *L'Archer de Charles IX* are — from the evidence of some indications in Part II (275, 276, 439) — fairly meritorious poetic achievements in their own right.

That Lucien is not the representative Poet but only, at very most, a symbol of the 'homme de poésie' is still further illustrated by the abnormal extent to which his character and personality are defined in relation to others. The impression

most often created of him by the novelist is that of the plaything
of circumstances, the instrument of others. Throughout *Illusions
perdues* he is a passive, rather than a creative or dynamic,
character. It is, for example, Sixte du Châtelet who for his own
advantage brings Lucien to Mme de Bargeton's notice (77). It
is Du Châtelet again who contrives for him to be spied on by
Chandour (149). It is Mme de Bargeton who insists on the
elopement to Paris (160) — immediately, without waiting another day for Ève's wedding. Du Châtelet persuades him to
return Mme de Bargeton's letters to her (200); Coralie puts
him to bed with her ('Lucien fut mis à son insu dans le lit de
Coralie': 314); the journalists supply him with his opinions
(247, 327, 345-348, etc.); Coralie urges him to change his
political allegiance (387); and so on. We see, therefore, that in
his characterization of Lucien, Balzac defines him negatively
rather than positively: by reaction away from his family, and
by endless suggestibility, rather than by the defined impulse
towards any consistently desired ideal.

There seems, in short, to be no core to Lucien's personality.
The force that propels him — especially through the Parisian
episodes — is the external force of pressure of events, not the
inner dynamism of his own character. And this fluctuating
uncertainty is admirably symbolized by the uncertainty over his
surname. Is it Chardon or De Rubempré? (Lucien is never
legally De Rubempré in the course of this novel, but obtains
the letters patent and legally becomes De Rubempré in *Splendeurs et misères des courtisanes*: *1*(6), p. 432.) Such ambivalence points to a deep-seated crisis of identity: an alienation
so marked that Lucien evidently cannot be regarded as representative of any family, social class, vocation or walk of life.
Such is his sexual ambivalence ('une jeune fille déguisée': 59;
'il avait les hanches conformées comme celles d'une femme':
59-60; 'son étrange beauté': 178, 'beau comme un dieu grec':
257; 'toutes ces natures à demi féminines': 448; 'ses petites
mains de femme': 571) that he cannot even be regarded as
representative of his own sex. Nevertheless, his is a distinctively
individuated character — negatively defined — passing through
a series of sharply focused and indeed skilfully articulated
events.

3

Contributory Causes of Lucien's Downfall

L ET us first consider, in severely tabular form, the interaction of journalism, the theatre, sex and politics in Lucien's catastrophic Parisian career. The key stages in his downfall are as follows:

---

p. 174: his separation from Mme de Bargeton, and hers from him (for which Balzac blames *him,* p. 201);

pp. 238-245: his growing involvement with journalism, and comparative abandonment of the Cénacle (cf. D'Arthez's sorrow: p. 245);

pp. 302-305: Lucien writes his review of *L'Alcade dans l'embarras*;

p. 315: Lucien becomes Coralie's lover (cf. p. 324: 'Une voix lui disait que, si Daniel avait aimé Coralie, il ne l'aurait pas acceptée avec Camusot'; cf. also, however, p. 342);

p. 326: 'Une sorte de pressentiment lui disait qu'il avait été serré sur le cœur de ses vrais amis pour la dernière fois'.

---

p. 349: Lucien writes his hostile review of Nathan's novel;

p. 364: Lucien writes his favourable review of the same book;

p. 364 (despite p. 342): *Lucien writes his wounding article about Du Châtelet and Mme de Bargeton*;

(p. 368: Lucien writes a review for and against Nathan's novel;)

p. 366: Lucien is dazzled by the Duc de Rhétoré's tempting words about the *ordonnance*;

p. 367: a conspiracy has already been mounted against him in high circles, inspired by the series of wounding articles — by Lucien and others — concerning Du Châtelet and Mme de Bargeton;

p. 377: Lucien's blasphemous baptism (cf. p. 360).

---

p. 380: 'il ne calcula plus';

p. 380: Mme d'Espard rebukes him for not coming to her house, and for cutting her at the Opéra;

p. 381: 'Initié aux trahisons et aux perfidies du journalisme, il ignorait celles du monde';

p. 383: mention of the *ordonnance*;

pp. 383-384: Mme d'Espard's warning;

p. 387: Coralie advises him to change his allegiance from Liberalism to Royalism;

pp. 387-388: Lucien will not desert Coralie for Mme de Bargeton;

p. 389: De Marsay's warning;

p. 392: Lucien's resolution to work is weakened by love.

---

p. 390: 'Le jeu devint une passion chez lui';

p. 393: Lucien and Coralie fall heavily into debt;

p. 410: he loses at the gaming-tables;

p. 414: Lucien defects to the Royalist newspaper, *Le Réveil*;

p. 415: he thus becomes an object of aversion to the Liberals;

pp. 415-416: publication of the sonnet ridiculing Lucien;

pp. 416-417: Lucien is blamed for Florine's desertion of Lousteau;

p. 417: Vernou detests Lucien because of p. 330;

p. 417: Lousteau loses a commission of 3,000 francs from Finot because Finot has to pay Matifat more for his sixth of the Liberal weekly than he need have done; thus Lucien has no friend except (p. 419) Martainville.

---

pp. 421-422: *Finot discovers from Des Lupeaulx that the Royalists have no wish to protect Lucien*;

p. 423: the *ordonnance* is a 'plaisanterie';

p. 426: on the eve of Coralie's appearance in a new play, D'Arthez's book is published;

p. 427: D'Arthez's book must be savaged by the Royalist press (despite the — to them unknown — fact that D'Arthez is a Royalist!), and Lucien must write the scathing review or else Coralie will suffer;

p. 428: Lucien writes the treacherous article, which (p. 429) D'Arthez corrects;

p. 429: Coralie's play is a failure, and she falls ill;

p. 430: Florine takes over her role;

p. 431: Finot suggests to Lucien the subject matter of an article lampooning the Minister of Justice (the Garde des Sceaux) and his wife.

---

p. 435: Lucien's sham *ordonnance* is torn up 'because of' this scurrilous satire;

p. 438: Lucien is wounded in a duel with Michel Chrestien (occasioned by the D'Arthez review);

p. 439: *L'Archer de Charles IX* is published by Fendant and Cavalier, but passes unnoticed;

p. 440: Coralie falls ill;

p. 442: *Lucien commits the forgeries*;

p. 443: Coralie dies;

p. 447: Lucien loses what little money he still has at gambling;

p. 448: Bérénice's self-prostitution;

p. 448: Lucien flees from the capital.

The first striking observation about this synopsis is its extreme complexity. And the clothing in further confusion and detail of an action already as complex as this in its bare outline is doubtless intended to convey to the reader an immediate impression of the bewilderment by which Lucien is stricken on the Parisian battlefield. Although he is almost always at the centre of the action in *Un Grand Homme de province à Paris* (not, however, on pages 421-423), a wealth of significant detail nevertheless escapes him.

Secondly, the synopsis shows that from page 435 until the end of *Un Grand Homme de province à Paris* Lucien is progressively overtaken by the inevitable consequences of his own actions. He had always acted, in Part II, without regard to the future — treating every circumstance as chance, and so failing either to comply with or to discern necessity. The *ordonnance*, the Royal letters patent granting him the official right to the surname and arms of De Rubempré, was always an elaborate hoax (unless Lucien was prepared to become Mme de Bargeton's lover); the perfect pretext for its not being granted occurs when Lucien writes his unfortunate article attacking the Garde des Sceaux. The duel with Michel Chrestien, brought about — indirectly — by the D'Arthez review (436, cf. 431, 446), is therefore the ironical consequence of Lucien's defection to the Royalists (itself occasioned by the hope of the *ordonnance*); more directly, the duel is occasioned by Lucien's awkwardness in assuming contradictory journalistic disguises. The fact that

the publication of *L'Archer de Charles IX* passes unnoticed
is the result of the same animosity of the Liberals towards
Lucien as had caused Finot to trick him into ridiculing a Cabinet minister.

Coralie's fatal illness appears to be the immediate consequence of her secret promise to return to Camusot (440); but
the underlying cause of this promise is the debt into which
she and Lucien have been led by the extravagance of the theatrical and journalistic worlds. Just as Lucien is the cause of
her final illness, so she is the cause of his reckless betrayal both
of D'Arthez and Liberalism. The threat, on page 422, that the
actress would be 'sifflée et sans rôles' if Lucien would not
'opter entre d'Arthez et Coralie: sa maîtresse était perdue s'il
n'égorgeait pas d'Arthez' (427) had caused him to write his
disloyal review of D'Arthez's book. Yet, by another ironical
twist of events, even after Lucien has betrayed D'Arthez, Coralie meets with such a hostile reception in her new play that she
falls ill. Having recovered from this illness, she is filled with the
ambition to outdo her rival Florine by surpassing herself in
the leading role in another play: 'Coralie outrepassa ses forces'
(440), and never recovers from the exhaustion brought on by
these physical and psychological pressures.

Moreover, Lucien's acts of forgery are the inevitable outcome of a situation in which both he (because of his duel, and
because of his estrangement from the Liberals) and Coralie
(because of her theatrical misfortunes) are penniless. The web
of interconnecting blunders, vanities and egoisms is complete
when Coralie dies and her lover returns to his birthplace. The
sequence of events is governed by a rigorous necessity to which
the flimsy make-believe of the theatre and the *demi-monde*
cannot blind the reader.

Viewed more broadly as a series of disastrous misjudge-
ments extending over seven months (September 1821-April
1822) rather than as the calamitous but painfully protracted
dénouement of six [1] months (April-October 1822: 435-448),

---

[1] Five, if we consider that Lucien is at Angoulême in September
1822 (547, 559).

Lucien's Parisian downfall can be seen to contain four essential elements: his uncertainty regarding his poetic vocation; his dazzlement by the prospect of social success; his temptation by journalism; and his involvement with Coralie. Yet not one of these factors in themselves would have produced a downfall of such magnitude as Lucien's. The uncertainty regarding his poetic vocation would simply have meant the abandonment of his work as a poet. His dazzlement by the prospect of social success might have led him to great worldly success, had he not been infatuated with Coralie. His involvement with Coralie might have been propitious to his poetic vocation, had he not been obsessed with the desire to rise in society. His conversion to journalism (not to insist on his desertion of one camp for another!) is certainly, in Balzac's eyes, tantamount to a downfall: a downfall which, to Lousteau (255, 332), is a damnation: and evidently a fate far worse than the conversion of anyone to mere social worldliness. Even so, journalism alone would not have produced the utter shipwreck of all Lucien's hopes — literary, social, sexual and financial — which is his fate in Paris. It is the integration of all these elements which gives each of them a potentiality for disaster that none possesses in itself.

Indeed, at least one of these four elements has in itself a potentiality for good. In one of the crucial passages in *Un Grand Homme de province à Paris* (315), Balzac stresses that Lucien's relationship with Coralie has a sanctifying quality. Being an expression of true love, it purifies and redeems the eighteen-year-old actress from her previous life of sexual degradation. The love of this young couple is a 'noble amour, qui réunissait les sens au cœur, et le cœur aux sens pour les exalter ensemble'. It is an 'absolution', a 'divinisation qui permet d'être deux ici-bas pour sentir, un seul dans le ciel pour aimer'. The polarization of male and female is transcended in the unity of two hearts. The implication is clear: just as this love absolves and sanctifies Coralie, so also it could have become the means of Lucien's purification and redemption, leading him homewards to his poetic vocation. The relationship with Coralie contributes to his downfall only because, by the time when he meets her, he appears to have lost his poetic vocation and not to wish to find it again. As a stepping-stone along the path of social ambition her help and advice are positively harmful. It is she, more than anyone else, who encourages Lucien to defect from the Liberals to the Royalists (387). Although enmeshed in the snares and delusions of the world, she is far less worldly-wise than her 'friend' and rival, Lousteau's mistress, Florine.

Conversely, except for the love-affair with Coralie every one of the four elements previously mentioned is a reflection of the crisis of personality — the accelerating collapse of his identity — which besets Lucien's life. Through Coralie he might, in other circumstances perhaps, have attained redemption in the form of a clearer self-awareness and the fulfilment of his gifts as a poet. But the reality is that he is an ambiguous being, half-male, half-female, half-poet, half-journalist, half-aristocratic, half-plebeian, who does not know himself, and the total collapse of whose identity is eventually symbolized by the forgeries.

One sharply focused incident will serve to illustrate this deepening crisis of individuality: Lucien's signature of his journalistic articles. He writes no less than three reviews of the second edition of Nathan's novel published by Dauriat (349, 364, 368), the first hostile, the second favourable, and the third weighing up the arguments for and against. We know from page 272 that, on his first reading of Nathan's novel (when it was still in its first edition), he had been deeply impressed by its qualities.

On page 345 Lousteau suggests that he should write a scathing review of the second edition of Nathan's book (a question of personal revenge: Lucien has just made the painful discovery that Dauriat has not even bothered to pretend to read his sonnets). Lucien's initial reaction to Lousteau's proposal is consistent with the praise expressed on page 272: 'Mais que peut-on dire contre ce livre? Il est beau'.

By page 359, however, after the writing of the masterly savage review ('un chef-d'œuvre où il n'y a ni un mot à retrancher, ni une ligne à ajouter': 349), Lucien's position has entirely changed. On page 349 he had, of course, perjured himself by writing something in which he did not believe. But by page 359 he has come to believe in what he had previously written (which was the diametrical opposite of his true beliefs). This reversal of attitude is emphasized in two separate exclamations: 'Les signatures ne m'inquiètent pas, dit Lucien ; mais je ne vois rien à dire en faveur du livre' (359); 'Mes amis, foi d'honnête homme, je suis incapable d'écrire deux mots d'éloge sur ce livre' (361). It is as if he has brainwashed himself into believing, no longer in the merits of the book, but in what he had written in his first (hostile) article. 'Tu pensais donc ce que tu as écrit? dit Hector [Merlin] à Lucien. —Oui' (359). Nevertheless, he also writes a favourable article (364) consonant with his true impressions based on an actual reading. Ironically, his third and final article (368) — a masterly summing-up of the arguments both for and against Nathan's novel — is merely prompted by a vain desire to show off his acrobatic (345) skills as a journalist. His article damning a show at the Théâtre de l'Ambigu-Comique, for entirely selfish reasons (369), is shortly afterwards sub-edited into an ingenious display of praise (367); to which he reacts both indignantly and with deep unselfconscious irony: 'Je comprends que je ne suis pas libre d'écrire ce que je pense' (368)!

At the very peak of Lucien's Parisian misfortunes his intensifying crisis of identity has one further serious result. A sudden proliferation of journalistic articles is directed against D'Arthez, anonymous articles with whose authorship Lucien is mistakenly credited (431). It is these articles, rather than the judiciously balanced one which D'Arthez had himself corrected (428-429), which sting Michel Chrestien into insulting Lucien (436), so provoking the duel. Likewise, the sudden crop of articles directed against Du Châtelet and Mme de Bargeton, the heron and the cuttlebone, has the direst consequences for Lucien; yet only one of these, the last (364), has come from his pen. In their desperate shortage of copy, newspapers are only too happy to use a profitable subject until it is threadbare. Such was the mockery of Du Châtelet and Mme de Bargeton, begun by Lousteau (304-305) writing under Lucien's inspiration, continued by Vernou (350), and pushed to new heights of savagery by Lucien himself — to whom, it seems (358), the previous articles have vaguely been attributed. In this case too, the ambivalence of Lucien's identity means that worse is attributed to him than he has actually done.

This article in which Lucien mercilessly attacks Du Châtelet and Mme de Bargeton brings us to the very crux of the human realities in *Illusions perdues*. His downfall is not simply the result of confusions of personal identity brought about by inadequacies of self-knowledge. Still less is it simply a consequence of the affair with Coralie. Lucien's plunge into the abyss is the work of Du Châtelet and Mme de Bargeton, his two fiercest enemies. More particularly, it is the work of Mme de Bargeton, who hates the young man because he has ceased to love her: in this act of revenge she is willingly abetted by Du Châtelet, whose overriding ambition is to discredit Lucien and to marry Mme de Bargeton himself. Whilst she seeks vengeance, he pursues calculation. And her vengeance springs from the darkest depths of the novel, her elopement with Lucien and separation from him.

It was she — as we have seen — who had peremptorily insisted on his accompanying her to Paris in Part I (160). Her removal to an apartment on the very first day of their arrival in the capital had been engineered by Du Châtelet (174). The more complete break, again encouraged by Du Châtelet, had come on page 201, when the young man had returned all her letters, enclosing with them a mordant letter of his own (201-202). Balzac, deliberately perhaps, is by no means clear in his apportionment of responsibility for these developments. He writes on page 201 (a little unfairly, it may be thought) that Lucien 'ne se dit pas qu'il avait, lui le premier, étourdiment renié son amour, sans savoir ce que deviendrait sa Louise à Paris'. Elsewhere, however, he comments: 'Il se préparait chez madame de Bargeton et chez Lucien un désenchantement sur eux-mêmes dont la cause était Paris' (179). Even so, Lucien's indignation — when deserted in Paris by a woman who had brought him there, who had even tiptoed away from him at the Opéra (195), and who in Paris was so much better protected than he — is not difficult to understand. The tables are turned on the woman who, with Mme d'Espard, had cut him in the Champs-Élysées on his first Sunday in the capital (198) when, two months later, he and Coralie cut these same two ladies in the Bois de Boulogne: 'le moment où il put échanger par un coup d'œil avec ces deux femmes quelques-unes des pensées de vengeance qu'elles lui avaient mises au cœur pour le ronger, fut un des plus doux de sa vie et décida peut-être de sa destinée' (320).

It is the humiliation caused to Mme de Bargeton — in her cousin's presence! — by this encounter, together with the largely mistaken attribution of the *Héron/Seiche* articles to her former admirer, and his rejection (387-388) of her overtures (380-384, 388), which fire her with that implacable, almost Racinian hatred which calculatingly ensnares the young man in the trap of social ambition, change of political party and the *ordonnance* (421-422). The nakedness of the motives which inspire the principal characters' actions and lead essentially to Lucien's failure is thus apparent. Only because of Mme de Bargeton's intense sexual frustration is Lucien destroyed by means of the subterfuge of the letters patent; his fellow journalists' jealousy of him would not have been enough. Only because of that other mainspring of human behaviour in the *Comédie humaine,* the imperative desire for money, does Lucien commit the acts of forgery which seal his disastrous Parisian career. The 'or et plaisir' by which Paris is characterized in the opening pages of *La Fille aux yeux d'or* (*1*(5), pp. 1039-1052) are at the very heart of the tragic chain-sequence of events in the second Part of *Illusions perdues.*

4

The Parisian Characters

Two features of Balzac's characterization stand out: his coupling of characters, so that each exists in relation to the other by contrast; and his close association of characters with their backgrounds, of time, place and circumstance.

The existence of polar opposites, starkly contrasting characters, in *Illusions perdues* is obvious enough: Lucien and David; Lucien and Daniel d'Arthez; Ève and David; Mme de Bargeton and Coralie; Florine and Coralie; the satellites of Mme de Bargeton at Angoulême, the satellites of Mme d'Espard in Paris; Mme de Bargeton and Mme d'Espard; the *Parisian* Mme de Bargeton and the *provincial* one; Finot and Martainville; the Liberal journalists and the Royalist ones. Within this range of dichotomies different contrasts can be seen. Some are the contrasts of types, other contrasts are more individualized. A *typical* contrast is that of the Parisian and Angoulême social circles. A more *individualized* contrast is that between Lucien and Daniel d'Arthez, or between Florine and Coralie. The Mme de Bargeton/Mme d'Espard dichotomy is more in the nature of a contrast between the provinces and Paris. The contrast within Mme de Bargeton herself, between the provincial woman of *Les Deux Poètes* and the Parisian woman of *Un Grand Home de province à Paris,* is less illustrative of her particular individuality than a reflection of the differing worlds in which she moves.

The very fact that Lucien is contrasted not only with David but also with D'Arthez (and even with Du Châtelet and Lousteau), and the fact that Coralie is contrasted both with Mme de Bargeton and with Florine, indicates also that in each of these dichotomies Balzac is contrasting not a total character but a facet of one. Thus, in the Lucien/Du Châtelet dichotomy Lu-

cien's naïveté and directionlessness are contrasted with Du
Châtelet's cunning and fixity of purpose; whereas in the Lucien/
David dichotomy the two young men — both being 'poets' —
appear equally naïve and their main points of contrast lie partly
in their steadfastness of purpose in pursuit of a poetic objective
and partly in their sincerity and family loyalty.

The case of Mme de Bargeton well illustrates Balzac's
technique of associating a character with its background to the
extent that the two become inseparable. Whenever we see Mme
de Bargeton (and, throughout Part II, her presence is admit-
tedly sensed rather than witnessed), we see her from the outside:
we are not shown the intimate workings of her mind. As a
character she seems only to interest Balzac in respect of her
connection with Lucien. Not even her relationship with Du
Châtelet can command the novelist's attention. To a remarkable
extent, she takes her colour from her surroundings. She *appears*
(at least) to be a different person in Paris from the person she
was at Angoulême; and this is because she is viewed against
two sharply differentiated backgrounds, the provinces and the
capital. In Part I she had always seemed out of place in Angoulême; but was it merely the eccentricity of the bluestocking
(71-72)? In Part II she is seen in her true light. No real evolution in her character occurs between Parts I and II. It is simply
that, in *Un Grand Homme de province à Paris,* there is now
a greater congruity between herself and her background than
had previously existed. Within only a few days of her arrival
in Paris, she has undergone a 'métamorphose' (198). 'Lucien
put voir Louise dans sa transformation, elle n'était pas recon-
naissable' (197-198). There has been no struggle to achieve this
profound change in her manners and appearance; it is as if she
has been changed by the wave of a magic wand. Within so
short a time of her removal to the capital, no trace of the
provincial woman seems to remain; and such traces as there
had been were in tiny details, such as her habit of carrying her
handkerchief in her hand (186)! Even at Angoulême she had
had that 'hauteur native d'une femme noble', that '*je ne sais
quoi* que l'on peut nommer *la race*' (186) which becomes her
saving grace in Paris. Balzac re-uses the word *metamorphosis*
on page 387: 'Louise aussi s'était métamorphosée! Elle était

redevenue ce qu'elle eût été sans son séjour en province, grande
dame'.

Before her arrival in Paris with Lucien in September 1821,
Mme de Bargeton had always lived in the provinces (70-73).
Balzac's reference to her as the 'grande dame' implies, therefore, that she was innately Parisian and that her thirty-six years'
sojourn at Angoulême had prevented her from revealing, or
fulfilling, the essence of herself. The woman who had been at
variance with her provincial surroundings now flourishes in a
congenial milieu. Her metamorphosis had been four months
more rapid than is suggested on page 387: almost, in fact,
instantaneous. Instead of a slow maturation of character, we
are shown the talismanic influence upon her of her exceedingly
distant (67) cousin by marriage Mme d'Espard — who, in
September 1821, following the withdrawal of Mme de Beau-
séant from Paris nineteen months previously (*Le Père Goriot;*
I(3), p. 265), has become the leader of fashionable society.

This suggestion by Balzac that the essence of Mme de Bargeton's character was Parisian does much to clarify the nature
of her relationship with Lucien, which in some respects —
especially concerning their separation in Paris — remains strik-
ingly mysterious. A 'grande dame', preoccupied with the values
of social worldliness, is what she fundamentally is. Her 'poetic'
face was a mere aspect of her provincial eccentricity, to satisfy
which Du Châtelet had introduced Lucien to her. Small wonder,
then, that forgetting his poetic achievements (the — to her —
contingent, rather than the essential, face of Lucien) she parted
from him so soon. Introduced to her as a poet, he had become
a physically admired man. Yet, sexually, he had remained
aloof! Their passion, which would otherwise have been fulfilled at Angoulême, had never found an outlet there (145-146).
Balzac does not comment on the fact, which nevertheless is
clear from the circumstances (195), that in Paris the relationship of Lucien and Mme de Bargeton is never sexually con-
summated.

Each, then, sees the other in relation to a changing background. The young man, or the woman, who had seemed so
attractive in Angoulême is much less so in Paris by comparison
with others. In relation to Mme de Bargeton, even on their very

first — and only — day together in Paris, Lucien 'comprit qu'il n'était plus le Lucien d'Angoulême' (173). To him, Mme de Bargeton always represents a social superiority — either to raise him up from the Houmeau to the Vieille-Ville at Angoulême, or to diminish his self-respect in the capital.

Du Châtelet is likewise presented against a changing background; but, being sure throughout the novel of his own identity (which Mme de Bargeton basically is from page 198 of Part II, and which Lucien never is), 'l'ex-beau de l'Empire' (338, cf. 551) merely appears out of his element in Angoulême. He is essentially a Parisian, yearning for and eventually reinstated within his true milieu: 'l'homme du monde au fait de la vie parisienne', 'élégant et à son aise comme un acteur qui retrouve les planches de son théâtre' (178). And he is never more a Parisian than when, in *Les Souffrances de l'inventeur,* he goes back to Charente as its prefect, this return symbolizing the only way in which Angoulême has ever existed for him: namely, in its relationship to Paris, and thereby to the centralized government of France. In terms of his contribution to the plot Du Châtelet is never presented introspectively but always through action. It is Du Châtelet who compromises Mme de Bargeton and Lucien at Angoulême, thereby forcing them to elope to Paris. In Paris, being in his true element, he takes control of the two would-be lovers, keeps them apart, persuades Lucien to return all Mme de Bargeton's letters, betrays the knowledge of Lucien's past to the dandies, and does everything to encourage Lucien along the deceptive path of the *ordonnance,* even to the extent of calling for him and taking him along to the Ministry of Justice on the day when the sham letters patent are torn to shreds before the young man's eyes. Although, however, fulfilling the role of a tempter figure, leading Lucien on to his undoing, Du Châtelet is not described in a Satanic light.

Coralie, a Jewess (293) like so many of Balzac's courtesans, has the beauty, warm-heartedness and spontaneity which he considered to be typical of her people; she lacks the astuteness of a (Gentile) Florine. In her love for Lucien she attains the perfect fulfilment of her individuality (this love being an 'absolution': 315), and yet does not repudiate that other *face,* or

aspect, of her life: the relationship with Camusot. This dual
relationship, partly venal and partly sincere — which was a
cliché of Romanticism [1] — does not impair her coherence as an
individualized type; it is, nevertheless, a remarkable fact. Lucien, we read (324), felt that 'si Daniel avait aimé Coralie, il
ne l'aurait pas acceptée avec Camusot'. But this sharing of
Coralie brings with it positive financial advantages. It is Camusot who provides the apartment in which the young lovers
live, and who finally (440) discharges the promissory notes for
which Lucien is held responsible after his publishers' bankruptcy. In her relationship with Lucien she is, it seems, true to
herself, although (inevitably, because of Camusot) not strictly
true to her lover.

According to the inexorable logic of Balzac's plot, she more
than anyone is responsible for the disasters which befall them
both: disasters created for themselves — through her rivalry
with Florine, the intrigue involving Matifat's share of the Liberal weekly (431), and Lucien's switch from Liberalism to
Royalism — in the wider worlds of the theatre, journalism and
politics. As an actress she is used to appearing before the
widest of Parisian worlds, the theatre; but, as an actress, she
also has two faces: the inner self and the theatrical mask.
This ability to superimpose an artificial identity upon her true
self is helpful to her, although not always entirely convincing
(334), in her relations with her two lovers. But it is also of the
greatest possible detriment to Lucien that she should encourage
him, not to strive to hammer out his own identity, but instead
to dissolve and destroy that identity beneath an endless suc-
cession of masks: 'Est-ce que je ne suis pas ce soir en Anda-
louse, demain ne me mettrai-je pas en bohémienne, un autre
jour en homme? Fais comme moi, donne-leur des grimaces
pour leur argent, et vivons heureux' (363). In strictly worldly
terms, there is no future for the relationship of Lucien and
Coralie. Loving him in solitude, precisely because it is true
love, incurs Mme de Bargeton's implacable hatred. And by

---

[1] Cf. the relationship of Flore Brazier with both Jean-Jacques
Rouget and Maxence Gilet in *La Rabouilleuse*.

encouraging him to go out into the world, and to seek the
ordonnance and marry a rich wife (387), she is bound to lose
him altogether.

Daniel d'Arthez and his Cénacle are the diametrical opposites of Lousteau, journalism and the theatre in that the
Cénacle is conscious of its strength and integrity, its true identity and undeviating fixity of purpose, whereas actresses (by
definition) have no professional identity but are as fickle — or
'mobile' (90, 134, 163, 193, 257) — as Lucien himself. 'La corruption de la chair, la corruption de l'esprit', Balzac wrote
(*4*(2), p. 374) of the sequel to *Illusions perdues, Splendeurs et
misères des courtisanes,* in terms which are equally applicable
to its forerunner. Lousteau and his fellow-journalists are also
play-actors, throwing attitudes and assuming masks for a financial consideration. The journalists, such as Lousteau and Lucien, are the lovers of the actresses, such as Florine and Coralie
— this in itself symbolizing the interpenetration of the corruption of the two worlds. It is not, however, implied by Balzac
that the journalists are unfaithful to their actress-mistresses in
the way in which these actresses — with their lovers' conni-
vance — are unfaithful to them. Indeed, the main cause of
Lucien's worldly misfortunes is precisely the fact that he will
not betray the purity of his relationship with Coralie by also
becoming Mme de Bargeton's lover.

The members of the Cénacle are even more varied in their
outlook and opinions than are the journalists: amongst the
various political viewpoints represented by its nine members,
Michel Chrestien is a Republican (who much later, in 1832,
will die fighting on the barricades of Saint-Merri: 228), whereas
there is no Republican journalist. However, they do not barter
their opinions for money, nor do they waver in their opinions
(412). So strong are they in their self-assurance that, like Félicien Vernou (360), they could even play-act for a time by
engaging in lucrative journalism, if by this means it were necessary to promote some laudable artistic purpose (238): Michel
Chrestien could, in other words, assume a mask without its
destroying or even damaging his fundamental integrity. But
whereas the journalist Vernou utters mocking words about
making the sign of the cross and invoking the Holy Ghost before

writing an advertising brochure (a clear reference to the sin
against the Holy Ghost, the sin against the deepest promptings
of one's heart: 360), Chrestien and his fellow-members of the
Cénacle all recognize the moral imperative to be true to their
— utterly divergent — beliefs. Collectively, they transcend dis-
cordance of opinion in the fellowship and unity of undying
friendship. How different again from the journalists, all of
whom are ready, if necessary, to betray their 'friends' in furtherance of self-interest!

The Cénacle are, therefore, shocked when one of their number, Lucien, not only dabbles in journalism but in their presence
is actually received into the pseudo-fellowship of Liberal journalism by means of a blasphemous baptism (377). At the opposite extreme to blasphemy, they are consistently presented
in *Un Grand Homme de province à Paris* in spiritual terms.
The word *Cénacle,* in current literary usage in 1838 since its
application by Sainte-Beuve, ten years previously, to Victor
Hugo's regular gatherings of artist friends at his home in the
Rue Notre-Dame-des-Champs, is the diminutive of the word
Cène, meaning the Last Supper. D'Arthez is a Christ-like figure;
Bianchon, Bridau, Giraud, Ridal etc. are his disciples. Lucien
is the Judas-figure, betraying his friend and master for financial
gain. The defence of D'Arthez is undertaken by Chrestien, who
fights a duel with Lucien (438) and who also seems to foresee
Lucien's act of disloyalty (235) and asks God to forgive him
(238). Jesus, likewise, was defended by St Peter in the Garden
of Gethsemane after His betrayal by Judas. The very surname
of Michel Chrestien recalls the Greek title of Jesus. Léon
Giraud predicts Lucien's act of disloyalty in words (236) rem-
iniscent of Jesus's prediction in Mark 14.30. Thus D'Arthez,
Chrestien and Giraud all bear passing resemblances to Jesus.
They occasionally use words similar to His. And they are
involved in scenes and situations which also remind us of
Him: of Judas's act of betrayal, the skirmish in the Garden
of Gethsemane, and the disciples gathered together for the Last
Supper in the upper room. D'Arthez's Christian name, Daniel,
has a strongly prophetic quality. Michel Chrestien's connotes
the strength of the archangel who defeated the dragon during

the War in Heaven. [2] Such Biblical allusions help to clothe the members of the Cénacle in a spiritual lustre which is 'not of this world'. Yet the Cénacle is not a doctrinally Christian fraternity. Bianchon does not believe in the immortality of the soul (228); Léon Giraud predicts the downfall both of Christianity and of the family (228). Chrestien's Christianity, with its emphasis upon political equality, is imbued with the teachings of Saint-Simonianism. Above all, Balzac's Biblical allusions add to the *sublimity* of D'Arthez and his followers, underlining the contrast between the journalists and them. These indirect quotations from the New, and occasionally the Old, Testaments are not metaphors or similes (though Balzac does now and again turn to the Bible for his imagery, as in the portrait of Coralie: 293-294). [3] Instead, the members of the Cénacle move and speak at times in the words of the Bible, like actors in the high spiritual drama which *Illusions perdues* essentially is.

Lousteau, in his great conversation with Lucien (245-256) and indeed elsewhere, is conscious of this spiritual dimension. It is the anguished consciousness of the fallen angel aware that he has fallen from bliss into inescapable perdition. In his first conversation with Lucien he tells of his 'désespoir du damné qui ne peut plus quitter l'Enfer' (255). 'On ne damne pas les démons', he exclaims bitterly to his companion on page 332. By page 428 this painful consciousness of damnation has been transmitted from Lousteau to Lucien, who, having to betray D'Arthez, says to the latter: 'laissez-moi dans mon enfer à mes occupations de damné'. Lousteau, too, is damned rather than damning, the doomed guide across the turbulent waters of the Parisian Inferno whose words are an unheeded warning.

Like the members of the Cénacle, the journalists are also strongly differentiated in their characterization. Lousteau is very different, for example, from Andoche Finot, although both men work for the Liberal Opposition press, one as a literary critic, the other as an editor and entrepreneur. Whereas Lousteau is even described as a poet (253), and clad in the Romantic

---

[2] Revelation 12.7-8.
[3] Cf. The Song of Solomon 4.4-5, 6.3-4.

melancholy of the Satan-figure in Vigny's 'Éloa', Finot (as the very pun on his surname suggests) is the archetype of the wily, calculating journalist-cum-businessman: a man who is not conscious of beauty when he sees it (as is Lousteau: 276), who is not aware of the promptings of goodness within the human heart, and who feels none of the remorse caused by disloyalty to a spiritual vocation. Finot is jovial, hail-fellow-well-met — and profoundly treacherous. The most notable instance of his treachery occurs on pages 421-422, in his conversation with Des Lupeaulx in (significantly enough!) a theatre foyer. In this scene Des Lupeaulx, a civil servant whose job it to determine which legal cases can go forward to the Court of Appeal, represents — broadly speaking — the Minister of Justice and, through him, the moderate Royalist Government. Finot ostensibly represents the Opposition press in which he has two stakes, one as the owner of a small Liberal daily (252, 290), the other as editor and joint owner (with Dauriat) of a Liberal weekly. Yet, despite this apparent conflict of interests and political loyalties between Des Lupeaulx and Finot, the fact which emerges from their conversation is that secretly they are on the same side. Having ascertained from Des Lupeaulx that the Governmental party has no wish to protect Lucien, its recent recruit, from the Liberals' attacks, Finot promises his opposite number that the turncoat will be discredited and crushed (422). Such collusion is by no means surprising in a devious journalist who had already declared: 'Peut-être serai-je ministériel ou ultra, je ne sais pas encore: mais je veux conserver, en dessous main, mes relations libérales' (286). Space precludes a closer study of Finot's acquisition of a two-thirds share in the Liberal weekly (273, 286, 327, 402-403, 416, 417, 422-423), which would well illustrate the extreme fluidity of his opinions — and that the side on which he and Des Lupeaulx are secretly ranged together is that of personal advantage.

Within the world of journalism the counterweight to Finot is Martainville. Whereas the former is ostensibly a Liberal, the later is genuinely a Royalist. And whereas the former is a fictional character, the latter actually existed in the pages of history — and, moreover, was one of the most notorious men

of his generation. Alphonse Martainville (1776-1830), playwright, dramatic critic and tireless campaigner on behalf of
the Ultra Right, had so outrageous a reputation that his very
appearance at a theatre could give rise to the threat of a public
disturbance. Both on political and on literary issues (such as
his defence of Shakespeare and Romanticism against the Liberal neo-Classical school) he was fearlessly provocative. The
accusation that he had betrayed his country by assisting the
passage of Blücher and his Prussian troops across the Seine
in 1814 — a completely unproven allegation — added still further to his notoriety. His outlook was so reactionary that *Le
Drapeau blanc*, the ultra-Conservative weekly founded and
edited by him, became an embarrassment to a more moderate
right-wing Government and eventually (in 1827) had to be
closed down. Such were the activities, in real life, of the man
— extreme in his attitudes, and suspected of duplicity — who,
in Balzac's universe of fiction, is the only genuine friend whom
Lucien ever has amongst the journalists. In the battle that rages
between the journalists after Lucien's defection, Martainville is
'le seul qui le servît sans arrière-pensée' (417), 'le seul qui le
défendît et l'aimât' (419).

It was a stroke of exceptional boldness, on Balzac's part,
to include a man as widely abhorred as Alphonse Martainville
within the fictional universe of *Un Grand Homme de province
à Paris*, thus juxtaposing the man guilty of duplicity and the
man suspected of it. Yet the playwright accused of 'betraying
his country' had never, in any case, betrayed his Royalism!
The gulf is a great one between Martainville's true and Lucien's
false Royalism, the former's courage and the latter's cowardice,
Martainville's out-Heroding consistency and the nebulousness
of Lucien's views. Was their bond of friendship primarily
sexual? Balzac gives strong indications that this may be so:
'La principale méchanceté des petits journaux fut d'accoupler
Lucien et Martainville. Le libéralisme les jeta dans les bras
l'un de l'autre. Cette amitié, fausse ou vraie...' (419). It is an
ironical reflection on the corruption both of the flesh and the
mind in the worlds of the theatre and journalism that the only
friendships which a man can form in those worlds are perhaps
based upon sexual attraction. There is, incidentally, no evidence

to suggest that the Martainville of real life had homosexual leanings.

Thus, in the great variety of Balzac's Parisian characters one from real life counterbalances the fictional Andoche Finot, whilst Lousteau's poetic consciousness of a Paradise Lost is offset by Finot's calculating astuteness; amongst the women, Mme de Bargeton's puzzling inconsistency is counterbalanced by the naïve, constant love of Coralie. Coralie does not have the perfection of an Ève Chardon because she is, for all her beauty and affectionate charm, a kept woman. The society ladies are actresses too, and far more ruthless and calculating than Coralie and even perhaps Florine. The poetic, though sadly fallen, Lousteau dreams — or used to dream — of a sublime love-affair with some fashionable woman: 'J'avais le cœur pur : j'ai pour maîtresse une actrice du Panorama-Dramatique [Florine], moi, qui rêvais de belles amours parmi les femmes les plus distinguées du grand monde!' (253). It takes Coralie to realize that, so far as Mme d'Espard and Mme de Bargeton are concerned, 'elles sont pires que nous' (358); Lousteau, it would seem, still harbours some illusions. Paris is not merely the meeting-ground of the noble and the ignoble writ large upon society, either as social ranks (the *noble* Marquise d'Espard, the *ignoble* Félicien Vernou) or as generalized moral attributes (the *noble* D'Arthez, the *ignoble* Finot). It is also the meeting-ground of the noble and the ignoble within each human heart. To an unusually intense degree Lucien is the connecting link between these extremes.

5

The Provincial Characters

IN *Illusions perdues,* as is not the case in many of Balzac's novels (*La Rabouilleuse* being an obvious parallel), Paris and the provinces are presented side by side and on an equal footing. Both stand in their own right, though each illustrates the other. Furthermore, Balzac emphasizes the links — mainly financial and administrative — which connect Angoulême and its inhabitants with the capital. One of his most characteristic themes as a novelist is that of the increasingly numerous exchanges between Paris and the provinces, in the aftermath of the Napoleonic centralization and as the economic and commercial ties fostered by the French industrial revolution bound them more closely together. In no other novel of the *Comédie humaine* does Balzac achieve a clearer composite picture of 'le triple mouvement qui amène de la province à Paris les poètes, les nobles et les bourgeois' (*4*(2), p. 139).

Because the provincial characters are presented side by side with the Parisian ones, and not viewed from the vantage-point of the capital, they are described in a sober light. Even David Séchard, the obviously 'poetic' exception in Angoulême, is so portrayed as to be markedly lacking in the intrinsic glamour of poetic genius. At most, in Part I (58-61), he shines with the reflected radiance of Lucien, whilst in Part III Balzac invests his laboratory (462-463) — and, still more so, his hiding-place at Basine Clerget's house (523) and temporary laboratory at his father's house at Marsac (525-526) — with the mysterious aura of some alchemist's work-room. It is hard for us to believe that anything so practical as a cheap method of paper manufacture, or a new method of sizing pulp in the vat, could come out of such mysterious retreats; and harder still to believe that Boniface and Jean Cointet could so readily have accepted that in that dark laboratory at Angoulême a new technological process was in the making (474, 488-489).

Although David's later and decisive sufferings are presented in Part III as being occasioned by Lucien and Paris, his initial and formative sufferings are created for him in Part I by his father and Angoulême. Just as David in his generosity of mind and heart is the very opposite of Balzac's typical provincial man, so old Séchard is the embodiment of a distinct provincial *type*. He is not, however, a monomaniac, for whilst the dominant trait in his character is avarice, a second trait — hardly less powerful — is drunkennesss. And the one 'passion' can be pressed into the service of the other, in that behind the mask of his drunkenness old Séchard is often more clear-headed than his business opponents think. As a businessman he is, indeed, extraordinarily clear-headed : a fact which the Cointets are the first to recognize (53, 531-532). He and the Cointets have exactly the same low provincial cunning whereby — as with the brothers' involvement of Métivier in their plans, seen through by old Séchard (531) — each side perfectly understands the intentions of the other.

In David and his father, Balzac has illustrated the clash of generations, a father and son whose outlooks and objectives are at variance. What separates the two is that most dominant of Balzacian leitmotifs : self-interest. It is in old Séchard's self-interest to starve his son of funds, so that the young man will work hard at his printing business and provide his father with a good rent. Old Séchard even retains the use of one room (49) or two (528) in his former home in which David now lives : David, on the other hand, adds on to the house in order to provide a home for Lucien. Old Séchard has deprived David of the 10,000 francs which were rightly his after his mother's death, this sum having constituted the mother's dowry (50, 137). David, on the other hand, makes allowance in his marriage settlement for an entirely notional dowry of 10,000 francs which he has not actually received from his bride and which he, in effect, gives her (161). Old Séchard has so little trust in his son that, even when he has seen with his own eyes the quality of the paper that can be made by the new methods, he will not advance the few thousand francs needed to secure David's release from his creditors (528). He is unwilling to make any gesture of confidence, or even of helpfulness, towards the future (504-505). In him Balzac develops a theme frequently explored in the *Comédie humaine:* that of the danger of not using wealth productively.

From this point of view, old Séchard is the diametrical opposite of the young journalists and actresses and indeed of Parisians generally. In their world money is squandered with careless abandon, in the pursuit of pleasure; in episodes such as that of the Liberal weekly Balzac reveals how that money is made. But Séchard's wealth is a private resource existing for no purpose beyond itself and its owner's personal satisfaction. Ironically, in order to justify his colossal egoism, he invokes what is to him the shibboleth of family responsibility. His duty, he claims, is towards the family in the second generation: 'que David s'en tire comme il pourra, moi je ne pense qu'à cet enfant-là' (513). Such (perhaps laudable) concern for family continuity and the transmission of family property cannot, however, blind us to old Séchard's patent insincerity in alleging this motive. Just as Lucien betrays his father, so old Séchard betrays his son. The miser's anxiety about his grandson is merely a device to shuffle off his more immediate responsibilities. 'Ce sera le fils qui enrichira le père. Quoique ce soit le monde renversé, cela se voit quelquefois' (138) is not just Balzac's wry comment on a particular situation but a reflection of what he seems to have regarded as a general social evil: the upheaval of traditional virtues, and the dissolution of the family unit by egoism.

Although — as old Séchard rightly sees — his son's common sense is certainly to be distrusted, David has a wife who does more than make up for whatever practical qualities he may lack. Ève reveals 'les symptômes d'un caractère viril' (92), and yet is truly feminine: 'douce, tendre et dévouée'. In her, as in her brother, masculine and feminine attributes are peculiarly intermingled. She is the deeply loving wife, the affectionate mother, the dutiful daughter-in-law and daughter, the energetic but inexperienced businesswoman, and the doting sister who, overcoming all her illusions concerning Lucien, becomes strong-minded enough to discern his faults. The contrast between

Ève and her husband is more subtle than that between herself
and Lucien. Whereas the interpenetration of male and female
characteristics in the two Chardon children is fairly simplistic,
Ève and her husband are truly complementary beings who
together form a perfectly functioning, and fruitful, whole. Lucien, compared with his sister and brother-in-law, combines
countless incompatible features of character within himself but
lacks the one quality (possessed by them in abundance!) which
would have enabled a distinct identity to assert itself: will-
power. Hence Ève's increasing respect for David as he persists
in his stubborn scientific efforts, whereas for Lucien, who is
deficient in the corresponding literary will-power, she comes
to feel nothing more than the love a man might feel for his
mistress, 'malgré les désastres qu'elle cause' (543). And so,
within the actual course of *Illusions perdues,* Lucien — like a
mistress, and unlike his sister and brother-in-law — gives birth
to no achievement of any value.

In her reduced social circumstances Lucien's mother has
become a midwife, helping others to give birth (55): a circumstance which gives rise to the cruel pun which the Bishop of
Angoulême unwittingly perpetrates against the young man at
his poetry-reading (119). A deeper significance in Mme Chardon's occupation as a midwife lies perhaps in the fact that,
belonging as she does to an ancient and noble family extin-
guished at the French Revolution, her new role as a midwife
and the wife of an inventor may symbolize a new and positive
function of aristocracy (seldom emphasized by Balzac): that of
bringing a new world into being. Even, however, when viewed
as a character divorced from symbolism, Mme Chardon may
not appear fully convincing to some readers. It is doubtful
whether, in purely historical terms, a Rubempré even in Rev-
olutionary times would have married a pharmacist and, when
widowed, taken to midwifery. In Mme Chardon Balzac describes a character whose way of life has certainly only been
made possible by the exceptional historical circumstances
through which she has lived: the turmoil of the French Revolution, and the confiscation of aristocratic estates, accounting
— fictionally, at least — for her gradual decline from a priv-
ileged social elite to the lower levels of the working class.

Incredibly enough, although the kinship of distant relatives is readily acknowledged in aristocratic circles (witness the case of Mme d'Espard and Mme de Bargeton), Mme Chardon does not appear to have any relatives who could exert a talismanic influence for the benefit of her son and daughter. Her importance in *Illusions perdues* is, therefore, primarily functional. As the only child of the last of the Comtes de Rubempré (433), she is, genealogically speaking, a heraldic heiress able to confer upon her son(s) the right to quarter the paternal arms with her own and to adopt her surname in addition to the father's; Lucien's father not having been armigerous, however, the *ordonnance* becomes necessary: this is no adoption of the maternal in addition to the paternal surname and arms, but the obliteration of the father's family by the mother's. [1]

If Mme Chardon's is a *rôle sacrifié,* the very reverse is true of Boniface and Jean Cointet, Pierre Petit-Claud and Cérizet. The Cointets, the up-and-coming printers and (it seems) the leading businessmen of Angoulême, form a pair of brothers in the sharpest contrast to David and Lucien — who, it should be noted, are still referred to as 'les deux frères' in Part III (567, 569). Whereas in the latter pair one brother is betrayed by the other, the two Cointets are the perfect foils for one another, each being complementary to the other person rather in the manner of David and Ève. When driving a bargain, Jean reinforces his elder brother's arguments in cruder terms (614-615). For the realists that they essentially are, they are perhaps unduly credulous with regard to David's scientific powers; but then, they are *peasant* realists, for whom the young man's experiments have virtually become an object of superstition. That they should believe in David (whereas his father does not: 529) is, of course, necessary for the unfolding of the plot. They do, however, pretend *not* to believe in him towards the end of the novel (620-623).

---

[1] In choosing the name of Rubempré, Balzac has alluded, with uncanny accuracy, to one of the most ancient of historical noble families in the territory which is now Belgium: the Mérodes, Princes de Rubempré and Princes de Grimberghe.

Clearly differentiated though the Cointets undoubtedly are,
it is nevertheless true that they are as much *types* as individuals.
This criticism, indeed, may be levelled — in greater or lesser
degree — at all the characters involved in the plot against David
at Angoulême. The Cointet brothers represent a type frequently
met with in the *Comédie humaine*. They are the energetic businessmen whose unflagging enterprise and ruthless cunning lead
them upwards towards ever greater prosperity and social prestige. Their acquisition of David's secrets, and their take-over
of his printing-presses, are the key to their success both in the
higher realms of commerce and in public life. A significant
factor in this success is that, even in the Angoulême days of
their career (which are all that we are really shown of Boniface
in *Illusions perdues*), the Cointets had managed to involve Paris
in their underhand dealings, thus bridging the gap between the
provinces and the metropolis and injecting into the Angoumois
something of the capital's dynamic impetus. How different they
are in this respect from both generations of Séchards!

There are three ways, in *Les Souffrances de l'inventeur,* in
which Paris impinges upon the Cointets' world: first, through
Lucien's acts of forgery which are the direct cause of David's
downfall and the indirect cause of the Cointets' success; secondly, through their involvement of their paper-merchant, Métivier, in the discounting of Lucien/David's bills; and thirdly,
through the fact that Petit-Claud, acting on the Cointets' behalf,
employs the unscrupulous services of Cérizet, 'l'ex-gamin de
Paris' (467), in his machinations against David. The impression
gained from Part III of *Illusions perdues* is that, whilst David
is locked in his self-imposed scientific seclusion and whilst Lucien has been (as it were) psychologically imprisoned within
Paris in a world of falsely glittering fantasy, the Cointets — in
perfect freedom — have been plying their trades of printer,
banker and discount-broker between Angoulême and the capital. Act I of the drama of their self-advancement is not complete
until page 605! Their second Act consists of the acquisition of
David's secrets (606), by which point the action of *Illusions
perdues* virtually ends. The events of Boniface Cointet's life
continue and ramify, however, far beyond the confines of the
substantive events of this novel: 'riche de plusieurs millions,

nommé député, le grand Cointet est pair de France, et sera, dit-on, ministre du commerce dans la prochaine combinaison. En 1842, il a épousé la fille d'un des hommes d'État les plus influents de la Dynastie, mademoiselle Popinot...' (624). Although extremely little is seen of Boniface elsewhere in the *Comédie humaine,* we read in *La Maison Nucingen (1(6),* p. 391) that the position of Cabinet minister has been achieved. His marriage to Mlle Popinot provides a chronological surprise, for it is quite evident from *Illusions perdues* that by 1842 the bridegroom must be at least fifty years old, whilst the bride — as both *César Birotteau* and *Le Cousin Pons* indicate — can only be about twenty.

But these last tremendous events in the elder Cointet's life (in so far as it is revealed to us by Balzac) are surely not to be taken entirely seriously. They are the last flourish of the Balzacian magic, as the novelist's wand connects Paris and the provinces more closely than ever through the union of a Cointet and a Popinot. Boniface Cointet, therefore, is both individual and type. The type is the stock figure of the parvenu millionaire risen from small provincial beginnings by devious paths. The individual — and the uppermost side of the character — is the closely observed Angoulême printer whose actions are soberly expounded and psychologically consistent.

Whereas, in the main, the Cointets are conceived of by Balzac as individuals rather than as types, Cérizet and Petit-Claud are cast far more obviously in certain *typical* moulds. Cérizet represents one distinct Parisian persona, the working-class urchin brought up in an atmosphere of crime and immorality, and therefore selfish and lacking in moral awareness. This again is a favourite theme of Balzac's: the amorality that has resulted from the increasingly masterful selfishness of mankind aggravated by a decline in religious sentiment and by the upheavals of the French Revolution. 'Cérizet avait importé les mœurs du gamin de Paris dans la capitale de l'Angoumois... Sa moralité, fille des cabarets parisiens, prit l'intérêt personnel pour unique loi' (467). Referred to not only as a 'gamin de Paris' (467, 470, 471, 578) and 'ex-gamin de Paris' (467, 578) but also as 'ce jeune Parisien' (467) and even as 'le Parisien' (569, 577, 578), he becomes at times symbolic of the depravity and corruption of Paris generally. The influence of this Parisian upon Angoulême is as corrosive as any acid. Just as Paris augments the Cointets' fortune and the sum of David's scientific knowledge (41, 43), so in its corruption both of Lucien and of Cérizet (both of whom betray their masters) it is pernicious in its effects.

Carefully examined, the turning-point in the delicately balanced plot of *Les Souffrances de l'inventeur* will be seen to depend upon Cérizet. Had it not been for Paris, therefore, the Cointets' and Petit-Claud's provincial plot would not have succeeded. The chain of events whereby David's secrets are snatched from him, the Cointets become millionaires, and Petit-Claud becomes a public prosecutor, turns on nothing less banal than Cérizet's seduction of a young laundrymaid. Once Cérizet has discovered that David is at Basine Clerget's (567), and has failed to apprehend him on the night when he came out to greet Lucien after the latter's triumphal banquet (567-568), it becomes imperative — if the bailiffs are to arrest David for debt — that he should be coaxed out of his hiding-place again. This is accomplished by means of the forged letter, purporting to come from Lucien, which Cérizet puts together for David (578). But how is David to be given this letter? The only possible method is for a genuine letter from Lucien to be replaced by this spurious one; and this replacement can occur only if a false message is given to Basine, persuading her to leave her house for a few minutes, during which the substitution can be effected. The instrument of these acts of deception is a laundrymaid whom Cérizet has seduced and made pregnant, Henriete Signol (576-579). In the episodic appearance of Henriette we see a further stage of moral depravity. Cérizet, having corrupted the provincial town of Angoulême, goes on to corrupt a girl of straitlaced moral upbringing who has come up to Angoulême from the countryside. As Cérizet uses on the girl he has already seduced all his blandishments to persuade her to deliver the forged letter, 'il y eut sans doute un combat où l'honnêteté d'Henriette se défendit pendant longtemps, car la promenade dura deux heures. Non seulement l'intérêt d'un enfant était en jeu, mais encore tout un avenir de bonheur, une fortune...' (579) At the heart, then, of this imbroglio are the familiar Balzacian motives of *l'or et le plaisir*: the potentially illegitimate child and a future of wealth and material happiness.

The letter delivered by Henriette to David in his concealment is yet another parallel between Paris and the provinces; for just as Lucien commits forgery in Paris, so Cérizet commits an act of forgery in producing this letter (578). Whereas, however, both Lucien and David pay the penalty for the former's acts of forgery, Cérizet gets away with his criminal action scot-free. The crime which is not considered or punished as a crime is one of Balzac's most central preoccupations; involved in this instance of an unexpiated crime is a lawyer. Like the barrister Fraisier in the much later *Le Cousin Pons,* the solicitor Petit-Claud both engages in illegal action himself and connives at criminal wrongdoing. He rightly recognizes that this forged letter is the cornerstone, and possibly the only cornerstone, on which he can build a prosperous career. David is lured out of his hiding-place, arrested, imprisoned, and forced to capitulate to the Cointets. As a reward for his complicity in these machinations Petit-Claud is given the hand in marriage of the heiress Françoise de La Haye (487-488, 535-536) and the promise of legal preferment (536).

But Petit-Claud refrains from committing forgery himself. The *Parisian,* Cérizet, forges in Part III in the provincial town just as the *provincial,* Lucien, forges in Part II in Paris. Petit-Claud connives at criminal wrongdoing to the extent that, whilst he does not suggest the perpetration of a forgery (577-578), neither does he do anything to bring the forger to justice. His first instinct, on discovery of the forged letter, is to keep it in his possession as a constantly available instrument of blackmail (610-611) — and so we are shown blackmail both in Paris (400-403) and in the provinces. This is the first aspect of Petit-Claud's contravention of the law, though the blackmail remains at the level of a brief threat (611-612). The one crime he actually commits is that, in relenting towards Cérizet, he destroys the criminal evidence on which society would have based a prosecution for forgery:

Je serai, dans trois ans d'ici, procureur du Roi à Angoulême, reprit Petit-Claud, tu pourras avoir besoin de moi,

songes-y. — C'est entendu, dit Cérizet. Mais vous ne me
connaissez pas: brûlez cette lettre devant moi, reprit-il,
fiez-vous à ma reconnaissance... Petit-Claud ne répondit
rien; il alluma une bougie et brûla la lettre en se disant:
— Il a sa fortune à faire! — Vous avez à vous une âme
damnée, dit le prote (612).

Thus, into this episode of the burning of criminal evidence
yet another favourite theme is introduced: the infernal pact,
already ingeniously developed in the encounter between Lucien and Herrera/Vautrin (584-603; cf. Chapter 6). In Balzac's
second treatment of this theme in *Les Souffrances de l'inventeur*
Petit-Claud is the 'master', Cérizet the 'slave': whereas the
master Herrera had ministered to the social advancement of his
slave Lucien, now in the relationship of Cérizet and Petit-Claud
it is the slave who ministers to his master's self-interest.

The very fact that this theme of the infernal pact occurs
twice within ten or eleven pages (602-612) is sufficient in itself
to suggest that, increasingly as the novel proceeds, Balzac
ceases to portray the *individual* in both Cérizet and Petit-Claud
and instead emphasizes the literary type. Petit-Claud may, in
the first place, have been modelled upon someone from real
life whom Balzac knew from his own two and a half years'
experience of working in lawyers' offices as a young man. There
are resemblances between him, Goupil in *Ursule Mirouët,* Vinet
in *Pierrette,* and Fraisier in *Le Cousin Pons*: in their voices
(*1*(3), p. 951; *1*(4), p. 71; *1*(7), p. 635), facial skin disorders
(*1*(3), p. 777; *1*(4), p. 71; *1*(7), pp. 635, 661) and viperine
appearance (*1*(3), pp. 935, 951; *1*(4), p. 71; *1*(7), p. 640). It
is not only in the physical sense, however, that Petit-Claud may
be regarded as a type rather than an individual. Through him
Balzac expresses all the essential features of his own view of
the law. We see Petit-Claud, for example, in unethical — although not illegal — collusion with the Cointets whilst purporting to act on his friend and client David Séchard's behalf. These
are the two faces of the law, the official and the clandestine.
Through Petit-Claud's skilful manipulation of the accumulating
promissory notes Balzac shows us how the civil law can be
used — just as the criminal law can be circumvented — in the

furtherance of injustice. The fact that Petit-Claud is a *provincial* solicitor is significant, and its significance is explained by Balzac at some length (486-487). For once, in the *Comédie humaine,* Paris is shown to be less corrupt than the provinces (and indeed, all Balzac's few virtuous lawyers, with the exceptions of Bongrand in *Ursule Mirouët* and Mathias in *Le Contrat de Mariage,* are in Paris): 'A Paris, un avoué remarquable, et il y en a beaucoup, comporte un peu des qualités qui distinguent le diplomate: le nombre des affaires, la grandeur des intérêts, l'étendue des questions qui lui sont confiées, le dispensent de voir dans la Procédure un moyen de fortune' (486). It is clear from this that the combination of a 'gamin de Paris' and a provincial solicitor will be invincible.

Petit-Claud, however, does not merely represent the profound corruption and venality of the legal system: he represents this aspect of the law only for as long as his plan remains unfulfilled and success out of reach. But as soon as he does achieve success, and once his 'infernal' pact with Cérizet has been made, Balzac resorts to the other (for him fundamental) aspect of the typology of the law: its contribution, by means understood only by itself, to the eventual triumph of justice. The law, therefore, is seen in two essential aspects: as a powerful agent in the perpetration of injustice, if used by the wrong hands, but as also developing a momentum of its own in order to ensure in some unfathomable way that right will eventually prevail. Viewed in one light (623-624), the law appears to contain within itself a redemptive force which will be the salvation of its own more dubious practitioners — but only when they have made their fortunes!

Thus, Petit-Claud embodies a philosophy of the law and of legal practice (provincial legal practice, in particular) which far outweighs any significance he may have as a personality in his own right. Likewise, Cérizet is not primarily considered as a personality in his own right, but as the Parisian traitor who betrays the poet David in Angoulême just as Lucien is the provincial traitor who betrays the poet Daniel in Paris. First and foremost, Cérizet is a symbol of the morally disintegrating influence of Paris; and he moves in *Illusions perdues* in equipoise to Lucien. The Cointet brothers are, however, more

strongly individualized. In fact, even the typological dénouement whereby Boniface Cointet becomes a deputy, a *pair de
France,* etc. is arguably, not the conventional *arriviste* ending
at all, but exemplary proof of the greatness — in both practical
and idealistic terms — of David's scientific triumph. David
himself is essentially *an* archetype of the Poet: *the* archetype,
indeed, of the Poet with will-power, and individualized to the
extent that the seed of his two scientific discoveries came from
Lucien's father. Ève, a physical seed of that father, is idealized
rather than individualized by Balzac to the extent that she
becomes all that could be desired in a woman (128). Lucien,
on the other hand, the provincial who becomes rootless both in
the provinces and in Paris, gives cause to doubt the truth of
Postel's remark that that same father 'faisait tout bien' (92). The
fact that Lucien, the prodigal son, is also the seed that 'fell by
the wayside' may in large measure be due to his mother, her
blind spoiling of him (544), and the profound ambiguity of his
part-plebeian, part-aristocratic birth.

6

Herrera/Vautrin

THE one remaining major character in *Illusions perdues* is the so-called 'Spanish priest' whom Lucien meets on a road just outside Angoulême as the former is (said to be) on his way from Madrid to Paris whilst the young poet is contemplating suicide. This meeting occurs on page 584 of the novel, only about forty pages from the end. But the importance of this priestly figure in *Illusions perdues* is not to be measured in terms of the number of pages he occupies in it, which is nineteen (584-603). The priest, who in fact is not a priest at all but an escaped convict, assumes a mythological importance in relation to which all the rest of the action must be judged.

The fact that the Abbé Carlos Herrera, for all his priestly and diplomatic pretensions, is really the escaped convict Vautrin (with whom readers of *Le Père Goriot* are familiar) is not something which Balzac chooses to make explicit to the reader of *Illusions perdues*. Not until page 597, close to the end of his episodic appearance, is he even referred to by his assumed name. Prior to this, he had been called 'ce voyageur, à tournure si patemment ecclésiastique' (584), 'l'inconnu' (584), 'le voyageur' (585), 'l'Espagnol' (585), 'le prêtre' (585), 'le chanoine de Tolède' (589), 'le prêtre espagnol' (589) and 'l'abbé' (592). Only in the sequel to *Illusions perdues — Splendeurs et misères des courtisanes —* does it become clear that Herrera and Vautrin are two faces of one and the same man.

The function of the spurious Spanish priest is twofold in *Illusions perdues*: to rescue Lucien from death, carry him away from Charente and (in *Splendeurs et misères des courtisanes*) launch him again on a career in Paris; but also to propound a view of life which is of deep significance to Lucien and to the *Comédie humaine* as a whole. Readers of *Le Père Goriot* will note the close resemblance of his remarks in that novel (*I*(3), pp. 135-146) to his analysis of the world here. For an analysis of the world generally, and the cogent expression of a philosophy of life, is what his near-monologue to Lucien essentially is: an analysis which draws, in support of itself, on a wide spectrum of historical reference, ranging from the rise to power and political influence of the adventurer Ernst Johann Biron during the reign of the Empress Anna Ivanovna of Russia (587-589), to an anecdote concerning Richelieu and Marshal d'Ancre (590), to the rise of the Medici family to the throne of the Grand Dukes of Tuscany (591), to Napoleon's alleged failure to do justice to Kellermann in his despatch on the Battle of Marengo (592). It is a strange and at first sight discordant register in which to speak to a young suicidal poet, but one that befits not only Herrera's alleged status as a diplomat but also Balzac's outlook on the world. Just as, in his moment of supreme crisis (424-425), Lucien's situation had been compared to Napoleon's, so now his future is viewed by the self-described Jesuit in worldly and heroic terms.

The fact that Herrera purports to be a Jesuit priest (597) is deeply significant. For at least two centuries, and especially since Pascal's condemnation of their order in the *Lettres provinciales,* the Jesuits had carried with them the imputation of worldliness and amorality. The doctrines that 'might is right' and that 'the end justifies the means' are for ever associated with them. They have also been accused of debasing the spiritual and sacramental qualities of Christianity by promoting their religion through political and diplomatic intrigue, and by pandering to the baser pleasure-loving instincts of men. It is these aspects of his so-called Christian faith which Herrera/Vautrin constantly emphasizes to Lucien: a faith which is in reality a system of amoral precepts, since — as he eventually admits (601) — 'c'est moi qui suis l'athée'. Any profession of belief in God is, therefore, a pretence: 'Je crois en Dieu, mais je crois bien plus en notre Ordre, et notre Ordre ne croit qu'au pouvoir temporel...' (597). According to this analysis, the temporal power is absolute, whilst Christianity (and here Balzac echoes a strong eighteenth-century philosophical tradition: hence, on page 601, the reference to Voltaire) is nothing more than a mythical system conveniently intended to keep the lower orders of society in subjection. The progression of Herrera's utterances on the subject of God is increasingly frank and secular. Beginning, on page 591, with the advice, 'Adorez comme Dieu même celui qui, placé plus haut que vous, peut vous être utile', he moves forward through an assertion of the primacy of the temporal power to a denial of any belief in the Godhead.

Herrera's analysis of human life is anti-metaphysical, being exclusively concerned with this world (which is, he implies, the only one). His precepts are not, therefore, founded upon any transcendent morality; they are presented as the dispassionate assessment of the ways of an imperfect world. They are observations which must be heeded if a man is to achieve worldly success — the only success that matters, and indeed (Herrera suggests) the only success that can exist for the vast majority of men. 'Les élus de Dieu sont en petit nombre. Il n'y a pas de choix : ou il faut aller au fond du cloître (et vous y retrouverez souvent le monde en petit!), ou il faut accepter ce code' (598). The corrupt and corrosive values of the secular world have penetrated even into the cloister. There is no clearcut distinction between 'spiritual' and 'material', 'right' and 'wrong'.

His observations are cynical. 'Aujourd'hui, chez vous, le succès est la raison suprême de toutes les actions, quelles qu'elles soient' (594) is the familiar Jesuit suggestion that might is right. 'Ne voyez dans les hommes, et surtout dans les femmes, que des instruments ; mais ne le leur laissez pas voir... N'ayez pas plus de souci de l'homme tombé que s'il n'avait jamais existé' (591): men and especially women are to be treated as merely means to an end, and (might being the only right) the weak and the unfortunate are unworthy of consideration. Yet Lucien is a fallen man, and Herrera takes an interest in him.

The fact that, despite superficial resemblances between his precepts and Jesuit doctrines, Herrera is not a Jesuit at all but an individual masquerading as a Jesuit is reflected in the basic dissimilarities between what he observes and teaches and what is taught by the Society of Jesus. The Jesuits, after all, were renowned for their loyalty and solidarity in the service of a religious ideal: an army fighting as one man. In Herrera, or rather in Herrera's view of the world, self-interest has made such advances that the battlefield is now viewed as a personal engagement between one man and the rest of society. Nevertheless, Herrera (seen in the light of the Jesuit symbolism) is seeking to recruit one further man to the army which will wage war against society at large. Although, according to Herrera, every man's struggles within society are for himself, Lucien — if he so chooses — need no longer struggle alone.

Both men, in their renewed assault upon Paris, are motivated by thoughts of revenge. 'Lucien revoyait Paris, il ressaisissait les rênes de la domination que ses mains inhabiles avaient lâchées, il se vengeait!' (599). Herrera/Vautrin's revenge, as is particularly clear from his attitude towards Rastignac in *Le Père Goriot*, is more in the nature of a vicarious triumph over the hypocritical forces of *might masquerading as right*, with the backing of the law, which have turned him into a social outcast. Lucien will become the *alter ego* through whom he, the convict and lucid analyst of a sham social system, will triumph over the world. 'J'étais seul, nous serons deux' (599) is Lucien's manner of viewing their collusion; in Herrera/Vautrin's eyes, there is only *one* person: and that person is himself! 'Ce jeune homme, dit l'inconnu, n'a plus rien de commun avec le poète qui vient de mourir. Je vous ai pêché, je vous ai rendu la vie, et vous m'appartenez comme la créature est au créateur.... comme le corps est à l'âme' (597): Herrera becomes a creator refashioning Lucien in his own would-be image, usurping the function of God Himself. The alliance of Lucien and this apparently holy man will be an unholy alliance because it means the total collapse of the young man's identity in the form of what is known to Christianity as the sin against the Holy Ghost. A Faustian pact, involving the surrender of the soul, will be signed. 'Si tu veux signer le pacte..., la diligence de Bordeaux portera quinze mille francs à ta sœur' (602). 'Mon père, je suis à vous, dit Lucien ébloui de ce flot d'or' (603).

Herrera/Vautrin's presentation to the reader of *Illusions perdues* as a sham priest is in harmony with the general message of the novel that the world is a place of delusion, hypocrisy and theatricality. It would be untrue to say that Balzac's Human rather than Divine Comedy is fundamentally God-less, though certainly religion (only represented by the Bishop of Angoulême in Part I and by the Abbé Marron in Part III, with no representative of it at all in Paris)[1] plays a conspicuously small part in this novel. Herrera himself is God-less, however, and just as he wishes to usurp the functions of God, so he usurps the priestly functions of spiritual teaching and moral judgement of the world. He has become a confessional figure to whom not only does Lucien confess but whose pronouncements have an objective categorical authority. The world he speaks of (from an outwardly spiritual and godly standpoint) is that of time rather than eternity, a world of human action and aspiration evolving through the generations. Herrera/Vautrin distinguishes between two kinds of history: 'l'Histoire officielle, menteuse, qu'on enseigne, l'Histoire *ad usum delphini;*[2] puis l'Histoire secrète, où sont les véritables causes des événements, une histoire honteuse' (590). Like himself, history has adopted a disguise: *secret* history (the only true history) masquerades as the *official* version. And it is because might masquerades as right (and so, in a world of delusion, *becomes* right) that secret history masquerades as (and *becomes*) the official history. Being concerned with human motives, secret history reveals the truth about the ruthless egoism of man, however much official history may disguise that egoism beneath altruistic overlays. It is characteristic of Herrera/Vautrin that he should deny the spiritual aspect of Joan of Arc's mission, emphasizing instead the folly of that mission (in diplomatic and *Realpolitik* terms) in that it prevented a united France and England from winning the mastery of the world. Similarly, he denies the spiritual and idealistic aspect of the Templars' achievement, imputing to that order the baser desire for worldly dominion: 'il s'était égalé au monde' (597).

To Lucien also he imputes the desire for worldly dominion: 'Vous voulez dominer le monde... Savez-vous pourquoi je vous

---

[1] Except for the nameless priest who makes a fleeting appearance at Coralie's deathbed (443, 445) and who presumably conducts her funeral service (446-447).

[2] 'For the Dauphin's use' (but not for his father, the King of France, who must know the *secret* history).

fais ce petit cours d'histoire? c'est que je vous crois une ambition démesurée' (591). And in this intuition he is right:
in *Un Grand Homme de province à Paris* the theme of Lucien's
desire to triumph over the world is a prominent one (196, 199,
256, etc.). Whether, however, he has the will-power to triumph
is another matter. It is significant that Herrera speaks to him
of domination *before* he corrupts him. Once his tempting overtures have been successful, he calls him — in the very last
words of the scene — 'un poète sans volonté' (603). Does Herrera even for a moment believe that Lucien is a stronger and
abler man than he really is? Arguably, all his words to the
young poet are a love-play designed to win himself a homosexual partner (for it is obvious from *Le Père Goriot* that
Vautrin is a homosexual: *1*(3), pp. 144, 186, 189, 192, 196,
203, etc.). In *Illusions perdues* Herrera/Vautrin is soon assuring
Lucien that his beauty far excels that of the young Biron (587);
smilingly, he twists Lucien's ear (592); 'Je vous aime assez
déjà', he confides on page 593; 'obéissez-moi comme une femme
obéit à son mari' (597), etc. And if indeed it is true that all
Herrera's words amount to nothing more than a love-play for
Lucien, then once again — in a context which is neither provincial nor Parisian, but universal — Balzac shows that the
whole of human life can be interpreted in terms of the two
primordial motives of *l'or et le plaisir*. For it is Herrera's
money which secures Lucien's consent to the 'pact'.

Certainly, it is difficult to believe that Herrera/Vautrin could
take Lucien seriously for any reason other than his extreme
physical beauty. His intellectual approach to the young man,
though it flatters the latter's vanity (593), is comically exag-
gerated to the point of hyperbole: 'Vous n'avez rien, vous êtes
dans la situation des Médicis, de Richelieu, de Napoléon au
début de leur ambition' (596); in this respect Herrera is even
more extreme than Balzac the narrator had been, towards the
end of Part II (424-425), in comparing Lucien to Napoléon. The
thought of Lucien, like Cosimo de'Medici, founding a dynasty
which would survive for more than three centuries surpasses all
credulity. Lucien seems, in fact, during this conversation with
Herrera more naïve and dull-witted than he has ever been. He
believes in an after-life to the extent that once he is dead he

may become (for whatever reason) an animal or a plant (586).
He has been 'condemned' to suicide by 'un tribunal souverain,
moi-même!' (586). His 'maladie incurable' is 'la pauvreté' (586).
'Lucien se prit à sourire en voyant ses pensées si bien devinées'
(591), never even beginning to suspect the depths of Herrera's
astuteness. He is artless in his astonishment at the breadth
of the older man's knowledge of the world: 'le chanoine connaît aussi le théâtre, se dit Lucien en lui-même' (601), and — a
sentence which caused Proust to comment on its 'gaieté vul-
gaire' and 'relent de jeunesse inculte' [3] — 'Allons, pensa Lucien,
il connaît la bouillotte' (596).

For his part, it can be argued, Herrera is merely playing
with Lucien through the medium of words. The digression on
national characteristics on page 600 is frankly a ludic display.
The story of the treaty-eating Biron, though true in its vaguest
outline, is so remote from Lucien's experience as to sound more
like an elaborate joke than a persuasive argument. The promise
'Ainsi, montez! nous vous trouverons un duché de Courlande
à Paris' (589) belongs to the realm of the Arabian Nights. As
to whether the remainder of Herrera's historical anecdotes are
'true' or are merely a dazzling word-game, the latter case is the
more probable: although the account of Napoleon's silence
concerning Kellermann's bravery at Marengo is substantially
true, that of the young Richelieu's tacit condemnation of Con-
cini to death is pure fabrication. Such word-games serve to
remind us that, in Herrera's view, the whole of life — like
bouillotte (596-597) — is a game and a pretence.

---

[3] M. Proust, *Contre Sainte-Beuve*, Paris 1978, p. 272.

7

Aspects of Narrative Technique

ILLUSIONS perdues is a narrative written in the third person: not (as are, for example, Benjamin Constant's *Adolphe* or Fromentin's *Dominique*) a first-person narrative presenting the subjective experience of one individual viewed from his point of view. Balzac consistently favoured the third-person narrative form, though the *Comédie humaine* contains several examples of first-person confessional narratives set within a wider, more objective framework; there are also *Le Lys dans la vallée* and *Mémoires de deux jeunes mariées,* both of which consist of an exchange of letters.

In *Illusions perdues* the third-person narrative form is no doubt chosen because a greater sense of objectivity, both psychological and historical, is thereby created. The narrator, standing above the action, can look into the recesses of his characters' hearts: thus, for example, recording the secret yearnings of Mme de Bargeton (71-73), the fact that Félicien Vernou is 'malade de son mariage, sans force pour abandonner femme et enfants' (329), and numerous interior monologues (272, 596, 608-609). The insertion of the overall action of *Illusions perdues* into an objective third-person narrative does not, however, preclude such a first-person confessional interlude as Lousteau's account of his early literary struggles in Paris (250-253). Generally, however, the circumstances of a character's previous life are conveyed in a flashback by the omniscient narrator (concerning old Séchard: 39-43, etc.; Mme de Bargeton: 67-70; Du Châtelet: 73-76) and by various skilfully interwoven flashbacks in the case of Lucien and David (54-56, 61, 63). The placing of details of Lousteau's earlier career into a narrative cast in first-person form serves both to stress the self-pity (251, 253, 255) in his attitude towards his

misfortunes and to impart a sterner tone to his warnings to
Lucien than any authorially detached narrator could have
given them.

As a narrator, Balzac both discloses and withholds, with
both a sense of humour and a sense of bitterness. Although the
comments of the omniscient narrator are often revealing, we
are, on the other hand, left in a state of ignorance concerning
Mme de Bargeton's true feelings towards Lucien at various
turning-points in the story. Did she elope with him out of
love, or because the duel had made it impossible for her to go
on living in Angoulême? Why does she consent to part from
him so abruptly in Paris? When Balzac, in his omniscience,
does explicitly comment on the latter crisis, his apportionment
of responsibility for the separation (201) perhaps comes as a
shock to the reader. But then, the reader is unable to form a
true judgement of the reasons for their parting, since the focus
of the action in *Un Grand Homme de province à Paris* is
practically always on Lucien himself. Balzac does not explicitly
comment on Mme de Bargeton's true feelings, or her lack of
self-awareness. Similarly, he does not explain what persuasion
Coralie brought to bear on Camusot on Lucien's behalf (440).
We are far removed from the narrative situation in (say) George
Eliot's *Middlemarch*, where four strands of plot — involving
the close personal and moral relationships of ten or so principal characters — are, though skilfully interwoven, nevertheless
independently sustained.

The narrator of *Illusions perdues* is also a person whose
private feelings of joy or sadness are not always kept under
severe restraint but are allowed to spill over into the narrative.
This is principally true of the comic element, although there
is the occasional authorial bitterness (557). In the main, however, we sense an exuberance, a revelling in the sheer excite-
ment of story-telling, which would surely not have been present
in a story couched in the first person — for, *Illusions perdues*
being essentially a tragedy, the sense of self-pity in Lucien's
personal narrative (as in Lousteau's) would have been uppermost. The ludic aspect of the Herrera narrative — dialogue,
not authorial discourse — has been discussed.

A further feature of the third-person narrative which would scarcely have been possible, had the narrative been written in the first person, is that the Balzacian narrator displays an insatiable hunger for encyclopaedic knowledge, and a desire to satisfy his readers' hunger for such information. The action of all three parts of *Illusions perdues* is presented against a background both of topography and history. Like Herrera, Balzac is eager to connect the personal experiences of particular characters — Lucien, the Cointets, Du Châtelet — with general social trends and patterns of human behaviour. His is a totalizing vision, intent upon seizing, and propounding, universal truths out of a profusion of specific circumstances. Whether in his account of the worlds of the law, finance, printing, paper manufacture, journalism or the theatre, or even in Herrera's unfolding of a philosophy of history, an encyclopaedic, expository purpose is evident. Balzac emerges as the social analyst, exploring the interrelationship of Paris and the provinces, and pondering the nature of the contemporary world.

This concern to expound universal truths, not simply about nineteenth-century France but about human nature generally, is perhaps the root cause of the innumerable apophthegms with which the text of *Illusions perdues* is studded: 'A force de parler, un homme finit par croire à ce qu'il dit' (487); 'Là où l'ambition commence, les naïfs sentiments cessent' (79); 'Travailler! n'est-ce pas la mort pour les âmes avides de jouissances?' (320); 'Après le vol vient toujours l'assassinat' (53); 'L'ivrognerie, comme l'étude, engraisse encore l'homme gras et maigrit l'homme maigre' (43); 'L'œil de pie est, suivant une observation de Napoléon, un indice d'improbité' (485). Such maxims and would-be proverbs also have their ludic aspect; and Balzac actually underlines their fallibility as generalizations by ironically listing a number of them (393) which are disastrous in their influence on Lucien's career, though observance of the same proverbs would not necessarily have the same disastrous consequences in the lives of other men.

In the pursuance of his desire to create a fictional world parallel to the 'real' world of history, Balzac introduces an enormous variety of characters into his novels and short stories. It has been calculated that there are altogether some 2,500 fictional characters in the *Comédie humaine* (*18*, p. 440. Cf. *1*(1), p. 18). *Illusions perdues* itself has 167 fictional characters — of whom 115, as against 166 in its sequel *Splendeurs et misères des courtisanes*, are recurring (*34*, p. 280). Except for *Splendeurs et misères des courtisanes*, no novel in the entire *Comédie humaine* has either more fictional characters or more recurring ones. And of the 265 recurring characters in the so-called 'Rubempré cycle', no less than 147 appear elsewhere in Balzac's universe (*25*, p. 82). In short, everything in *Illusions perdues* is conceived on the vastest scale. Not only are many of its characters envisaged as types rather than individuals (embodiments of general rather than particular truths), but the destinies of many more are further considered in other works. Far from being (like *Gobseck, Honorine* or *Autre Étude de femme*) a story or a series of stories within a frame, *Illusions perdues* bursts out of every frame that might be used to contain it. It is the matrix of numerous destinities, some explored — and some unexplored — elsewhere in the novels of the *Comédie humaine*. This is the meaning of the astonishing statement on page 606, well over nine-tenths of the way through the novel, that Act II scene 1 of the Cointets' drama has now been reached!

With reference to *Les Deux Poètes* and *Un Grand Homme de province à Paris,* Chapters 2 and 4 have already underlined Balzac's skill in interweaving patterns of resemblance and opposition. *Les Souffrances de l'inventeur* presents further parallels and contrasts. Lucien's prodigal-son return (539-540, 542) contrasts with his deceptive triumph engineered by Petit-Claud (545-550, 555-556, 562-564). The pact between Petit-Claud and Cérizet (578, 612) — an unwritten one — contrasts with the written contract setting out the terms of the Cointets' business association with David (615-616, 622-623). Between *Un Grand Homme de province à Paris* and *Les Souffrances de l'inventeur* the parallels are no less vivid. There is the parallel between Lucien's forgery of David's signature on the three promissory notes (442) and Cérizet's forgery of the letter (578) purporting to come from Lucien to David. There is also the parallel between Finot's manipulation of the Liberal press in Paris (286, 422-423) and Petit-Claud's manipulation of the Liberal press

in Angoulême (568-569, 612), with the further point of resemblance that both men engage in shady transactions with the
Royalist camp. Between *Les Deux Poètes* and *Les Souffrances
de l'inventeur* Mme de Bargeton's boudoir serves both as a
link binding beginning and end together and as a reminder of
the decline in Lucien's fortunes: the room where he was surprised by Chandour and Du Châtelet at Mme de Bargeton's
feet (149) is also the room in which he momentarily regains the
affection and loyalty of the woman who is now Mme Du Châtelet (573-574). In Part III the important events in the relationship of Lucien and Louise take place not in the Préfecture but
at the house which is still known as the Hôtel de Bargeton
(550): the dinner party which the young man was to have
attended at the Préfecture (547, 575) he, in fact, never attends.
Likewise, within *Un Grand Homme de province à Paris*, D'Arthez's initiation of Lucien into the high-minded literary aspira-
tions of himself and the Cénacle (220-224) is paralleled — within
two months — by Lousteau's initiation of him into other, almost
diametrically opposed mysteries of the Parisian literary life
(250-256); both initiations take place in the Jardins du Luxem-
bourg. Within *Les Deux Poètes* the scene of Lucien's poetry-
reading (99-123) is paralleled by that of David's courtship of
Ève (123-133): the settings, on this occasion, are different, but
— according to the internal chronology of the novel — the
events are simultaneous.

The creation of such contrasting scenes, occurring at similar
times or in similar places, means that, in the intervals between
them, the action often moves forward with bewildering rapidity.
About five weeks elapse, for example, between pages 238 and
244. Balzac must constantly modify the rhythm of his narrative,
and not only because of the necessities of interlocking the great
scenes: the sharp contrasts in the tempo of the action cor-
respond, at a much deeper level, to psychological imperatives.
The rapid pace of events in Paris intensifies Lucien's dreamlike disorientation. It is also in stark contrast with the slow
effluxion of time at Angoulême. This contrast illustrates a profound difference in the mental outlook of Balzac's Parisian and
provincial characters. On the battlefield of Parisian life, caught
in the cross-fire between Liberal and Royalist newspapers,

Lucien has only to make one false move and irreparable disaster will ensue; hence, during his Parisian crisis, the reference to Napoleon (424). In committing the forgeries the young poet makes such a fatal move in the thick of battle. Part III is then largely devoted to showing how the Cointets and Petit-Claud slowly and relentlessly turn this hasty folly to their own advantage.

Balzac's audacity in modulating the tempo of the action leads, at times, to chronological improbability — and even to certain inconsistencies in the dovetailing of Parts II and III. It is frankly improbable, for example, that all that is described by Balzac in pages 245-315 should have occurred in a single evening: a fact reflected in the admission (295) that more seemed to have happened to Lucien that evening than during the previous eighteen years of his life. Equally improbable, but this time more definitely situated in the area of melodrama, is the arrival of the 15,000 francs from Lucien and Herrera just as David has signed away his equity in the exploitation of his commercial secrets (617-618).

Not only does Balzac now and again pass judgement on his characters — as in his condemnation of Lucien for the breakdown of the affair with Louise (201) or his castigation of Camusot's cowardice (316) — but also the characters themselves comment from time to time on each other's behaviour (478-480, 623). What is most striking about the management of the narrative discourse is, however, the novelist's reticence concerning some essentials, his reluctance to alert the reader to the existence — still less, the significance! — of the more ironical juxtapositions of events. The narrator himself does not, for instance, underline the ironical parallel between Lucien's and Cérizet's acts of forgery; D'Arthez, in his letter to Ève, comes closest to doing so without exactly foreseeing that Lucien would resort to crime (480). The 10,000 francs which old Séchard refuses to pass on to David on his wife's death (50, 137) is the precise amount which David notionally acknowledges as his bride's dowry in their marriage settlement (161): it can hardly be a coincidence on the novelist's part that these sums are identical, yet the reader is left to make the connection and to draw his own conclusions. Again, Balzac does not stress the (already

sufficiently obvious) parallel between the *ordonnance* which
Lucien fails to obtain (383, 423, 433, 435) and the raising of
Mme de Bargeton's elderly father to the peerage with the
prospective reversion of his name and arms of De Nègrepelisse
to her first-born son (554). Du Châtelet, likewise, has simply
appropriated a nobiliary particle (73) long before that particle
is confirmed to him in the letters patent granting him the title
of count and nominating him prefect of Charente (435); the
point is not emphasized. There is a similar lack of explicitness
concerning the significance of the passage describing Coralie's
sanctification by true love (315). All in all, Balzac is tantaliz-
ingly selective in applying and releasing the pressure of authorial emphasis.

8

Chance and Necessity

L UCIEN'S encounter with Herrera/Vautrin on the highway
north of Angoulême is one of the great 'hasards' of which
Illusions perdues is full; or so it would appear, except that all
these 'hasards' have been contrived by the novelist. Proust, who
praises it both in his own words and in opinions attributed to
Charlus,[1] was especially struck by the beauty of this scene.
It is a scene in which ineluctable necessity is combined with
the highest imaginable unexpectedness of chance as Lucien
meets Herrera, they drive together past the Château de Rastignac, and Herrera explains to his travelling companion the
rigorous and undeviating laws which govern the achievement
of any worldly success.

The word 'hasard' abounds in *Illusions perdues*. For example, 'Quand le hasard fit rencontrer les deux camarades de
collège' (56); 'Par hasard, madame de Bargeton se mit à la
croisée pour réfléchir à sa position, et vit partir le vieux dandy'
(173); 'Par un hasard favorable, madame Chardon gardait la
femme du premier Substitut' (516): as these quotations indicate,
by no means all the 'hasards' in *Illusions perdues* are favourable
occurrences; indeed, the chance circumstance of Mme Chardon's acting as midwife to Mme Milaud is the only explicit
reference to a 'hasard favorable' in the whole of the novel.
Especially in *Un Grand Homme de province à Paris,* Balzac
— foreshadowing Baudelaire — creates an impression of the
omnipresence of chance and coincidence in the modern city
(211). 'Aujourd'hui, pour réussir, il est nécessaire d'avoir des

---

[1] M. Proust, *Contre Sainte-Beuve,* Paris 1978, p. 274; and *A la
recherche du temps perdu,* vol. II, Paris 1963, *Sodome et Gomorrhe,*
p. 1050.

relations. Tout est hasard, vous le voyez': these words of
Lousteau (277) are a sombre reminder to us, if not also to
Lucien, of how far the latter has travelled since his arrival in
Paris. Armed with *Les Marguerites* and *L'Archer de Charles IX*,
Lucien had come to the capital trusting in the *necessity* of the
recognition of his poetic merit. Yet, as Lousteau and his other
journalist friends explain to him, in Paris the recognition of
merit will not of necessity be meted out to any poetic work,
however self-evidently great. The capital bestows its fickle
recognition of merit, often for wholly adventitious reasons,
upon the man.

Nevertheless, Balzac is also at pains to emphasize in *Illusions perdues* that belief in, and reliance upon, the unaided
unfolding of chance is also an illusion; for in Paris — as indeed
in Angoulême — a hidden necessity reigns. Success comes reg-
ularly to those (like Du Châtelet) who, manipulating chance,
turn it into necessity. The measure of Du Châtelet's cunning
and of Lucien's simple-mindedness is seen, within only a few
days of the young man's arrival in Paris, in his displeasure
at the fact that Du Châtelet is there also: 'il maudissait le
hasard qui l'avait conduit à Paris' (177). Such contrivance so
well contrived as to appear the natural outcome of chance
— art, as it were, imitating nature — is the distinguishing mark
of the truly calculating man. Lucien, on the other hand,
although an artist in literary terms, is far too artless to pre-
arrange such 'chances' — or even to take advantage of chances,
unplanned by him, when they arise. Encouraged by the flat-
tering reassurances of those around him, 'il se dit vaguement
que Paris était la capitale du hasard, et il crut au hasard pour
un moment' (201). In him such a belief is nebulous and inter-
mittent, whereas Du Châtelet never ceases to believe in Paris
as the great arena of providential coincidence and to act on
the belief. Although, therefore, *Illusions perdues* creates a
dazzling impression of the multifarious workings of chance in
Parisian life, narratively it also conveys the countervailing impression that its hero is doomed.

Even more noticeable than Balzac's use of the word 'hasard'
to suggest this multifariousness of chance is his use of 'devait'

and similar words — especially in Parts II and III — to convey a sense of ultimate, or impending, disaster. The omniscient narrator, looking into his hero's future, permits no illusion of eventual triumph. Thus, Balzac foreshadows 'les terribles émotions du Jeu qui, plus tard, devait trouver en lui une de ses victimes' (322). Further examples in *Un Grand Homme de province à Paris* are to be found on pages 356 and 381. In *Les Souffrances de l'inventeur* there are similar authorial predictions: 'Lucien devait être et fut le jouet de Petit-Claud' (556); 'une poignée de main qui devait être la dernière' (575); 'Le plan de Cérizet... devait réussir' (576). Ringing the changes on this prophetic use of the imperfect tense of the verb *devoir* are other devices of the same kind: the imperfect tense of *aller* (118, 145, 552); the adjective 'dernier' on page 160 and elsewhere; the 'Il fut le Lucien de Rubempré qui pendant plusieurs mois brilla' of page 321; and the breathless 'comme on va le voir', favoured in Part III (461, 484, 510). Warnings delivered by other characters and the forebodings of Lucien's friends also point the way to disaster (389, 164, 235). The hero is even endowed by Balzac with a physical predisposition to failure (442).

An adjective, 'fatal', reinforces the noun 'hasard' and the verb *devoir* in Balzac's subtle interweaving of chance and necessity. Not only do these words interact with one another, there is also an interplay of shades of meaning within the adjective and the verb considered independently. 'Fatal' has the alternative meanings of *disastrous* and *inevitable*: pointing, in other words, both into the future (with all the disastrous consequences which will flow from the fatal thing) and into the past (indicating that the fatal thing was bound to occur or be). In the first sense Balzac refers, for example, to 'la fatale puissance de la Presse' (358); and in the second, which is less often found in *Illusions perdues,* he describes Mme de Bargeton as 'cette femme née pour être célèbre, maintenue dans l'obscurité par de fatales circonstances' (66): the 'circonstances', it seems, are *inevitable* rather than *disastrous* — although, as if by a miracle, Mme de Bargeton does manage to escape from them. Even in this provincial instance, however, there is a certain degree of ambiguity; and the interplay of meaning is all the greater in the (more numerous) Parisian instances. The tone of disaster is uppermost on, for example, pages 201 and 427, whilst the sense of *inevitable* predominates over *disastrous* — with the additional connotation of *irrevocably decisive* — when Balzac generalizes: 'tout homme, à moins d'être né riche, a donc ce qu'il faut appeler sa fatale semaine' (424 [2]). The generalizing use of 'fatal' on page 424 implies that, for men in general, there is the possibility — or 'hasard' — of things developing either for good or ill. But no such openness as to the future applies to Lucien in Balzac's particularizing application of the adjective to him in the now suppressed chapter-heading. This is because, throughout *Un Grand Homme de province à Paris,* Balzac has denied hope to Lucien by other narrative means. As if the hopelessness had not already been sufficiently emphasized, he (again on the same page!) fuses both the fateful and fatal aspects of the young poet's destiny by means of the comparison with Napoleon.

Just as the adjective 'fatal' contains within itself the interplay of two — if not three — meanings, so the verb *devait* connotes both the inevitability of the future and the inviolable laws governing a man's behaviour in the present. These laws are either the general laws relating to society at large or else the psychological necessities flowing from a man's individual human nature. 'Ce poète, qui ne devait réfléchir que sous le poids du malheur' (373) is both a projection into the future and (more significantly) a generalization based upon the previously described events in Lucien's life and upon the necessities of his psychological make-up; likewise with 'il y eut dans son salut [Des Lupeaulx's] un semblant d'amitié qui devait tromper Lucien' (386). Such uses of *devait,* Janus-like, point both to

---

[2] The words 'cette fatale semaine' were echoed in one of the original chapter-headings of *Un Grand Homme de province à Paris,* 'La Fatale semaine', cut out by Balzac's publishers in 1843 on the republication of *Illusions perdues* in the collective edition of the *Comédie humaine.* This title would occur on page 424, immediately before the words 'Dans la vie des ambitieux...', if chapter-headings were printed in the Garnier Flammarion edition.

the future and the past. At other times Balzac achieves this Janus-like effect through the juxtaposition of *hasard* and *devait*. 'Sa fortune ne dépendrait plus alors que d'un hasard auquel aiderait sa beauté... Étienne avait préparé pour Lucien un piège horrible où cet enfant devait se prendre et succomber' (420). Here, the references to the future and the past do not reinforce one another (as when the *devait* founded upon the past can be extrapolated into the future); they point instead in diametrically opposite directions. The 'hasard' of page 420 coaxes us briefly into sharing Lucien's hopefulness. The 'devait', after scarcely a moment's basking in this pretended good fortune, is like a sledgehammer blow from Balzac crushing hope and hastening 'cet enfant' onwards to the inevitable disaster. Once, indeed, chance — or the Fates? — seem to smile down on Lucien: 'ainsi, par la bénédiction du hasard, aucun enseignement ne manquait à Lucien sur la pente du précipice où il devait tomber' (313); but, as soon as they smile, Balzac — making himself into his own providential instrument — is there to illuminate the remorseless path that lies ahead.

The verb *devait* is not much used in *Les Deux Poètes* by comparison with the two later books. When, on page 146, it is applied to Mme de Bargeton ('ainsi, madame de Bargeton devait rester toujours visible'), it has the meaning of an unalterable necessity emanating from the social conventions of the past: not the narrative foreshadowing of a predestined future. For the consummation of her love for Lucien she is constantly, in the later part of *Les Deux Poètes*, on the look-out for a favourable opportunity (or 'hasard'). But, what with her husband's and servants' casual wanderings about the house, visits from outside intended either to prevent or to spy on the fulfilment of her love, and the fact that she has no small country property to retreat to (145-147), such a favourable opportunity never arises; she has even been reduced to thoughts of taking Lucien with her to her father's seat at Escarbas (146). Du Châtelet, likewise, is on the look-out for a favourable opportunity, the same one in fact for which Mme de Bargeton and Lucien are looking: the 'hasard' which would permit a closer physical expression of their love. But just as Mme de Bargeton is initially

unsuccessful in finding this opportunity, so Du Châtelet (necessarily) is also. Both strive to wrest from the provinces the
'hasard' which provincial life so seldom gives. When eventually
Chandour and Du Châtelet surprise Lucien *in flagrante delicto*
(how different this provincial 'immorality' is from the lasci-
viousness of Paris!), the ways in which such a rarely vouchsafed
'hasard' can be turned to one's personal advantage are remarkably demonstrated by Du Châtelet.

The duel to which Bargeton *necessarily* challenges Chandour, and on which the plot turns, is one of Balzac's most
favoured illustrations of the workings of chance. Du Châtelet
is 'heureux de ce duel qui pouvait rendre madame de Bargeton
veuve en lui interdisant d'épouser Lucien, la cause du duel'
(154). Yet behind this 'chance' lurks a deeper necessity; for,
whatever the outcome of the duel, Mme de Bargeton and
Lucien can no longer achieve the fulfilment of their love in
Angoulême. Perhaps unexpectedly, Bargeton wins. But all that
this means, in practical terms, to his wife is that Angoulême
— thanks to the tittle-tattling of Du Châtelet and Chandour —
has polarized into two camps and that her social prestige has
been compromised (158). Hence the elopement to Paris, the
logical extension of her earlier plan to withdraw to Escarbas.
Not having found the 'hasard' for which she had looked so
hard (or rather, having found it only to discover that the same
'hasard' had been found by Du Châtelet), she spurns provincial
necessity in the defiant escape from Angoulême to the great
city of 'hasard', Paris. Du Châtelet, after so easily dominating
these earlier chance occurrences, naturally pursues the 'hasard'
of the elopement which, viewed in another way, was a *necessity*
if ever Lucien and Mme de Bargeton were to become lovers.
By following them to Paris, he is able even there — with all
the vaster opportunities of 'hasard' at their disposal — to prevent them from becoming lovers; with the result that the love
of Lucien and Mme de Bargeton is never fulfilled, neither in
the town of necessity nor in the city of chance, whilst in Paris
Du Châtelet finally becomes Mme de Bargeton's husband and
from Paris they eventually return — as Parisians (having mas-
tered chance) — to Angoulême. A return to Angoulême is some-

thing she had never envisaged (158); yet, with Du Châtelet, she is able to return to her old haunts in triumph.

The Angoulême of Part III is no different from that of Part I except that in this new Angoulême Paris is no longer a dreamed-of future but a past shaping and influencing the provincial town. In the Balzacian universe one of the subtle interrelationships between capital and provinces is that totally unexpected strokes of chance rain in upon sleepy provincial towns from the metropolis: one such stroke of chance is Lucien's forgery of the promissory notes. Cérizet, like Du Châtelet but at a much inferior social level, is a masterly seizer of opportunities; and both these men originate from Paris. Cérizet indeed, as was noted in Chapter V, is the very type or embodiment of the Parisian proletariat. It is Cérizet, the Parisian in Angoulême, who forges Lucien's letter (578); and Cérizet again who sets the Henriette Signol episode in motion: 'après, Cérizet attendait tout du hasard' (579). And because, by means of the letter delivered by Henriette, David is inveigled out of his hiding-place and arrested, chance works in Cérizet's favour.

But, as befits the city from which Du Châtelet and Cérizet have sprung, it is Paris — rather than the provinces — which is the great theatre of chance. Parisians rely on the benevolence of chance to bring them to the top of the great social wheel. Finot does not shrink from any social cataclysm that would bring him personal success (287). Duelling is an even larger feature of Parisian life than it is of life in Angoulême. 'J'aurai peut-être un duel demain', Finot nonchalantly boasts (287). 'Je fais et signe d'un F un article foudroyant contre deux danseuses qui ont des généraux pour amis': the civilian — trusting in luck — is not, it seems, afraid of the military man! When Du Châtelet is aggrieved by one of the articles written against him, he comes to Finot's office to seek satisfaction, but quails before the prospect of a duel with Philippe Bridau (338). This is a 'hasard' of which Du Châtelet may not be able to take advantage! Significantly, only Lucien is actually wounded as the result of any threat of a Parisian duel (438), despite the fact that his seconds, Rastignac and De Marsay, have done their best to provide him with suitable weapons: 'Je vous promets que nous avons aidé le hasard: vous avez des pistolets de cavalerie' (438). Gambling is another major feature of Parisian life, and one which is altogether absent from Angoulême. As Lucien's fortunes become more precarious, he relies more and more upon the prospect of chance showering him with gold (322, 390, 391, 392, 409, 410, 431), unsuccessfully however. Lousteau also risks a bet, and loses (374). The money he loses is Lucien's, and it is money which Lucien never recovers except, when home again in Angoulême, in the form of smart Parisian clothes (558, 560, 561).

Clothes are as much a stake in the Parisian lottery as are *écus* and francs. In his initial attempts to scale the social heights of the capital Lucien undergoes no less than four changes of clothing (177-178, 180-181, 184, 196-197, 201), each more elegant than the last until eventually he is the perfect Parisian dandy. 'Un jeune homme mis ainsi', he is reassured by the leading Parisian tailor, 'peut s'aller promener aux Tuileries; il épousera une riche Anglaise au bout de quinze jours' (200). Even towards the very end of his Parisian misfortunes, Lucien trusts in his beauty and elegance to see him through all difficulties (420). But Camusot, who trusts in 'les hasards de la vie parisienne' (334) in order to win back Coralie, has based his protection of the young actress on something more solid — and, it would appear, more lasting — than elegance and physical beauty: 'quelque grands que soient les talents de monsieur, ils ne peuvent pas te donner une existence' (334). His wealth may perhaps have been amassed thanks to favourable 'hasards' in the past. But it seems now (or so he believes) to be above the depredations of Fate, except in so far as his money — like Matifat's in the affair of the Liberal weekly — is subject to the inroads made into it by the exploiters of physical passion. Sexual passion itself, though one of the great 'hasards', is also the most irresistible of necessities. Lucien meets Coralie by chance (except that, in the small world of journalism and the theatre, he must meet her sooner or later). Her love for him is presented as something overwhelming, however, like some psycho-physical attraction of mesmerism which no one can resist (292).

The theatrical world in which Lucien and Coralie meet is perhaps the greatest metaphor of chance and necessity. Again, apart from a brief reference to the provincial theatre on the last page of the novel, this is a world which does not exist in or near Angoulême. It is the microcosm of Paris as the great theatre of chance, a world in which Lucien, with his fine costumes and journalistic assumption of masks, becomes one of the most colourful actors. There are, however, two theatrical worlds: those epitomized by Coralie and Florine. Coralie's is confined to the professional theatre and fails to understand the real necessities of social life. Florine's radiates from the professional theatre outwards: as in the Matifat episode, she is always intent upon seizing a 'hasard', which is the inner necessity of success in Paris. Her lover Lousteau resembles her in this: play-acting even outside journalism and the theatre, he is the 'roi secret' (300) of the orgy which Matifat ostensibly provides. Lucien, on the other hand, resembles his mistress Coralie in her naïveté: they play-act successfully only within the theatrical world. However, the play-acting of the great world outside the theatre is performed according to different rules — as the *ordonnance* episode bitterly illustrates.

Magic and dream are the attributes of the theatre. They also radiate out of the theatre to envelop the whole of Paris. Even Angoulême is subject to the apparent intrusion of dream and magic. 'Lucien ... voyageait d'étonnements en étonnements' (284), 'volant au-dessus du monde' (292), in a world of theatrical 'enchantements' (292). Outside the theatre doors Coralie and he later give a supper-party which has 'l'apparence d'un rêve' (372), as if summoned into being by a magic 'coup de baguette' (372): it is a world functioning 'comme par enchantement' (373) except that it is financed on short-term credit by Camusot. Like something out of the Arabian Nights — or the theatre — Coralie's apartment is a 'palais des Songes. Lucien songeait presque' (373). Yet 'par moments il lui prenait des inquiétudes comme aux gens qui, tout en rêvant, se savent endormis' (373). The magical and dreamlike aspect of Angoulême is more fitful, but equally contrived. As Lucien and Petit-Claud walk home from the banquet held in the former's honour, 'en ce moment David se montra comme par enchantement. Voici pourquoi ...' (565) Later, surprised by the fact that Cérizet has sufficient money to buy his printing-business, '— Mais c'est de la magie,

dit David en demandant à Petit-Claud l'explication de ce
bonheur. — Non, c'est bien simple, les négociants de l'Houmeau
veulent fonder un journal, dit Petit-Claud' (616).

Although, however, the magic is equally contrived in both
worlds (and equally explainable in terms of selfish calculation),
Paris and the provinces differ markedly in respect of the dream
element. In *Les Souffrances de l'inventeur* the dreamer of Angoulême is David, the scientist who knows that the inanimate
world (at least) does not operate by magic but according to
rigorous scientific laws; and he is as stubborn in pursuit of the
fulfilment of his dream as ever Du Châtelet was in *Les Deux
Poètes* (147): 'ces hasards-là ne sont rencontrés que par les
audacieux chercheurs des causes naturelles!' (502) The dream
world inhabited by Lucien in *Un Grand Homme de province
à Paris* is, on the other hand, divorced from the realm of necessity. Fancying itself above necessity, it is in reality a retreat
from it. Hence the frequent occurrence of the Arabian-Nights
imagery of sultan and slave (191, 296, 354-355, 364, 365), with
its delusory suggestions of unlimited power. The power of the
theatre to suggest luxury and enchantment is strictly limited.
After Lucien's dream-like spell (297), two hours long, cast upon
him by his first visit to the Théâtre du Panorama-Dramatique,
'à la féerie de la scène, au spectacle des loges pleines de jolies
femmes, aux étourdissantes lumières, à la splendide magie des
décorations et des costumes neufs succédaient le froid, l'horreur,
l'obscurité, le vide. Ce fut hideux' (297). The reality behind the
dreamlike trappings of the Panorama-Dramatique is clear, certainly to the reader and seemingly at times to Lucien himself.
The reality behind the dreamlike trappings of Paris, though
equally clear to us, is undoubtedly not clear to him. As the
weeks elapse for him in the capital, the apparently magical ups
and downs of his Parisian career increasingly resemble the
twists and turns of some theatrical performance. Just as in a
play the apparent 'hasards' of the performance are subject to
an inner foreordained necessity, so Lucien is subject to a necessity, which however he fails to recognize. Hence the irony of
Petit-Claud's astute remark in *Les Souffrances de l'inventeur:*
'ce n'est pas un poète, ce garçon-là, c'est un roman continuel'
(610). If this is so, then the strangest of the 'hasards' which may

be held to disfigure *Illusions perdues* — such as Lucien's return to Angoulême on the back of the Du Châtelets' carriage (453-454), or the fact that after he has written his damning review of D'Arthez's book Coralie still falls ill and has to abandon her play (429-430) — simply emphasize that the hero of *Illusions perdues* is a fiction within a fiction.

9

Historical Reality

'ON commence à comprendre que je suis beaucoup plus historien que romancier', Balzac remarked in a letter to Mme Hanska (*4*(2), p. 595) written less than two years after the completion of *Illusions perdues*. He often voiced his ambition to write, through the medium of fiction, the history of contemporary France. 'Je le tiens', wrote Anatole France,[1] 'pour le plus grand historien de la France moderne qui vit tout entière dans son œuvre immense'. What contribution does *Illusions perdues* make to this historical record, and how accurate is it?

Before beginning *Illusions perdues* Balzac had visited Angoulême twice.[2] He paid no further visits there because the friends with whom he stayed moved away from the town in October 1834. These friends, however, were contacted by Balzac, at the time of writing *Les Deux Poètes,* for details concerning the topography of Angoulême: which information, including a sketch map of the streets, they obligingly sent him by return of post.[3] The writer Albéric Second, on whom the character of Lucien may partly have been modelled, has left an account of his chance meetings with Balzac in Angoulême; as one who had been brought up in the town, he comments on the reliability of the novelist's topographical knowledge — with the one, but major, reservation[4] that the Hôtel de Bargeton should not have been placed in the Rue du Minage (79). However, Balzac is principally concerned to stress the symbolic contrast between the Vieille-Ville, where Mme de Bargeton

---

[1] A. France, *La Vie littéraire,* 4e série, Paris 1892, p. 320.

[2] 17 July-22 August 1832; mid-April-c. 20 May 1833.

[3] H. de Balzac, *Correspondance,* vol. III, Paris 1964, pp. 114-115; Zulma Carraud to Balzac, 28 June 1836.

[4] A. Second, *Le Tiroir aux souvenirs,* Paris 1886, p. 19.

lives, and the Houmeau, at the foot of the hill, where Lucien lives at the outset of the story; and the Rue du Minage is
in the Vieille-Ville. Lucien moves to the old town, at the top
of the hill, when David gives him a home.

A similar topographical interest is evident in Balzac's treatment of Paris, especially in his description of the Galeries de
Bois (263-268). Between the time of Lucien's first visit to the
Galeries de Bois (in November 1821) and Balzac's time of
writing this passage (late in 1838), this strange and squalid
assemblage of booths and shops, a meeting-place for all classes
of Parisian society, had (in 1828) been pulled down. Balzac is,
therefore, supplying a historical record of what the Galeries de
Bois were like at a time when the unique character of these
buildings had become a rapidly receding memory. He is,
however, inaccurate in his remark that they continued in existence until 1830 (265). He regrets their demolition, with an
antiquary's lingering affection for the vanished past (268). It
is in Dauriat's shop, situated in the Galeries de Bois, that
Lucien glimpses two — Foy and Benjamin Constant (277) — of
the very few historical personages whom Balzac has briefly
introduced into *Illusions perdues*; others, also in *Un Grand
Homme de province à Paris,* being Talma (211) and Alphonse
Martainville.

The world of the Parisian theatres is conjured up with some
feeling for the character of each. Out of the ten or so Parisian
theatres then (1821-1822) in existence, Balzac refers to six. At
the Théâtre du Vaudeville Lucien is cold-shouldered by his
former journalistic colleagues (417); there, too, his downfall is
planned by Finot and Des Lupeaulx (421-422). At the Théâtre
du Gymnase Coralie makes her last stage appearance (429).
But it is at the Panorama-Dramatique, which in November
1821 was no more than seven months old, that Lucien experiences his magically enchanted evening (278-298). Balzac al-
ludes to the difficulties experienced by this fledgeling theatre
(279), but without mentioning the harshest restriction under
which it laboured: that it was not allowed to have more than
two speaking actors on stage at any one time. Indeed, he tends
to play down the very real legal and administrative obstacles
that were placed in its way. It was these obstacles which in

April 1823 caused the theatre to go bankrupt. Balzac notes the bankruptcy (410), but places it in March 1822.

A more serious criticism levelled against Balzac's historical accuracy concerns the press. M. Jean Gaulmier (*30,* p. 83) takes him to task for not causing his journalists to refer to the Press Law of 3 December 1821 during their various discussions (308-312, 379-380, 412-413). But the discussion on pages 308-312 takes place in November 1821, that on pages 379-380 in December, whilst the discussion on pages 412-413 occurs in the following March. Only the lesser discussions in December 1821 and March 1822 could have taken note of the statute of 3 December. Likewise, only the third discussion could have referred to Villèle's second Press Law (of 7 February 1822) as an accomplished fact (*30,* p. 84).

These considerations suggest that *Illusions perdues* does not reproduce the superficial appearance of history. Not only does it contain very few historical characters, but the predominantly imaginary characters are set against a background which, whilst being recognizably of its age, does not slavishly attempt to chronicle the salient political events of the passing months. It is sufficiently remarkable in itself that Balzac introduces into his narrative the actual historical names of newspapers, both Royalist and Liberal, even though he situates the foundation of *Le Réveil* in March 1822 (393, 414) when in reality it was founded on 1 August of that year.

From *Illusions perdues* Balzac hoped that an impression of representative truth would emerge. 'Le fait vient trop souvent démentir la fiction à laquelle on voudrait croire, pour qu'on puisse se permettre de représenter le jeune homme autrement qu'il n'est au dix-neuvième siècle' (88). Although his characters are for the most part entirely fictional beings, the novelist professes respect for the truth of the 'real' world which would belie any excesses of his imagination. It may be wondered, however, whether he is always respectful of the truth of this 'real' world. The fact that an escaped convict is travelling along the highway between Angoulême and Poitiers in the autumn of 1822, disguised as a Jesuit priest and diplomat, need not detain us; for Herrera/Vautrin so obviously belongs to the realm of myth. It is, on the other hand, significant that at this historical period intensive diplomatic negotiations were proceeding between Ferdinand VII and Louis XVIII with a view to the re-establishment of the Spanish king's absolute power. But what of the 'genuine', as opposed to the 'sham' diplomat, the German minister who attends the lavish supper-party in Florine's apartment and bandies pleasantries with the actresses and journalists (308-313)? Perhaps the *demi-monde* of Balzac's universe has penetrated the upper world of diplomacy and politics to a far greater extent than was actually the case in French society. The whole of this upper social world may well be distorted in Balzac's vision: doubt has been expressed, in Chapter 5, concerning the historical credibility of Mme Chardon.

One aspect of the private world of *Illusions perdues* which directly impinges upon the actual world of history is Balzac's social criticism. Counterbalancing the possibly far-fetched picture of legal corruption, which according to him is greater in the provinces than it is in Paris (486-487, 508-509), are various strictures on the procedures of the law. Balzac shows how the legal expenses of the protesting of promissory notes can artificially be piled up in order to reduce a debtor, such as David Séchard, to submission (491-492, 497-498). He even puts forward the practical suggestion that a law should be passed forbidding solicitors to spend more money in recovering a debt than the size of the debt itself (510). He complains, and supports his complaint with demonstration, that the so-called improvement patent was 'la plaie des inventeurs, en France' (516). He even comments on the low standard of Parisian hotels (170). But, above all, he points to the many difficulties faced by the young writer in Paris when he is trying to make his reputation.

The Parisian world described in *Illusions perdues* is largely a world of artists and of failed artists who have become reviewers. In the sphere of literary and theatrical reviewing Lucien rapidly becomes a journalist of a rare order. It is also implied that he has shamefully misused a rare poetic talent. But to what extent does Lucien's career symbolize the disasters that can befall the rare poetic talent in nineteenth-century Paris? As if to prove the extent of his true genius Balzac not only

supplies the text of the *Alcade dans l'embarras* review, brilliant
in itself (302-304), but also the texts of four of his sonnets from
Les Marguerites: sonnets composed at the novelist's request
by Charles Lassailly (247, 248-249), Delphine de Girardin (248)
and Théophile Gautier (249-250), competent if not great poets
of the day. They are of no higher quality than the anonymous
sonnet (415-416) — also Lassailly's work — by which Lucien's
enemies denigrate him. Other young poets of the early nineteenth century, Hugo for example, established their reputations
in the face of critical and public hostility. In view of the
mediocre nature of Lucien's poetic achievement, does Balzac
(as György Lukács suggests) present the archetypal history of
the young Poet of genius battling vainly against a Philistine
commercial world — or rather the historically less absolute
story of a second-rate versifier who, in the testing-place of genius, is weighed in the poetic balance and found wanting?

10

Conclusion

ILLUSIONS perdues is founded upon five important premisses, one of these being that 'les nuances si tranchées dans les Départements disparaissent dans le grand mouvement de Paris' (52). Paris has an identity and an essence quite different from those of provincial life. According to the German minister (308), it is the canker from which France — which not even the armies ranged against Napoleon could entirely subdue — may eventually die. And its death, if this does occur, will be due to the corruption of journalism. The most pernicious aspect of this corruption is that the journalist can strike deadly blows at his enemies from a distance (often the blows of mockery), in the full irresponsibility of the knowledge that he will never be held to account. His most savage blows are, though perhaps lethal, not strictly criminal at all: which is why Claude Vignon argues that a law must be passed to prohibit such a dangerous power (379). Journalistic abuse is a prime example of that favourite preoccupation of Balzac, the crime which is not a crime: it is 'comme un duel avec un absent, tué à distance avec le tuyau d'une plume, comme si le journaliste avait la puissance fantastique accordée aux désirs de ceux qui possèdent des talismans dans les contes arabes' (364).

The interaction of chance and necessity is the second of the fundamental premisses upon which *Illusions perdues* is built. The pattern of Lucien's life in *Un Grand Homme de province à Paris* is to come to terms with 'toutes les fangeuses nécessités de Paris' (372). These necessities are the product of 'l'intérêt accroupi dans tous les coins' (370). Not even literary and theatrical success is left to the chance reactions of readers and audiences, but is manufactured in advance (372). The failure of Coralie's performance at the Théâtre du Gymnase (429), despite the efforts of Braulard's claque (426), is the result of a complex interaction of necessities. The losing of illusions involves the recognition of these and all other necessities.

Prominent amongst the necessities is the exercise of talismanic power. This power, which is almost magical, appears to cut across the ordinary necessities of life. It also illustrates the Janus aspect of chance and necessity, since it is by chance that a man is able to invoke such power, yet that power becomes a necessity if he is able to invoke it. Indeed, even the 'chance' invoking of talismanic power has a twofold aspect, for a multiplicity of chances becomes almost tantamount to a necessity: 'à Paris, il n'y a de hasard que pour les gens extrêmement répandus' (211). Mme d'Espard wields talismanic power such that Mme de Bargeton 's'était dit qu'elle parviendrait en se faisant le satellite de cet astre' (187). People admitted to her circle enjoy great influence and prestige. Mme de Bargeton is admitted to it because of distant cousinship by marriage. Lucien is initially excluded from it by Mme d'Espard and Mme de Bargeton (195) and, when wooed by them, spurns them out of revenge (320). Talismanic power is the power which never fails, but Lucien is singularly clumsy in detecting where such power lies. He is inclined to find it in journalism (364), where in a manner of speaking it resides, or in his youthful vigour and beauty (383), or in the *ordonnance* (420). Du Châtelet has a far clearer perception of where the true talismanic power is to be found, and of how it can be tapped.

Mme de Bargeton's would-be talismanic protection of Lucien is inspired by love, but a love which, like his, will become revengeful if thwarted. This again is a fundamental premiss of the novel. Love, or 'passion', is the basic *hasard* of human life. 'Par quel hasard le protégez-vous?' Mme d'Espard asks Mme de Bargeton about Lucien (196). But it is chance which becomes a necessity in that the impact of such love is (generally) irresistible. We read that none of the schemings of the journalists and others gives evidence of any profound intellect or far-sighted planning: 'leur machiavélisme va pour ainsi dire au jour le jour, et consiste ... à épier les moments où la passion leur livre un homme' (367).

Herrera/Vautrin is another talismanic power, the supreme embodiment of talismanic power in *Illusions perdues*; and one encountered by chance, on the highway between Angoulême and Ruffec — the supreme manifestation of chance in the novel. Again, the exercise of talismanic power is inspired by love (this time, however, a love which is homosexual rather than heterosexual). And again, the chance of this encounter with the source of great talismanic power will become a necessity, in that Lucien's worldly success will be founded upon Herrera's secret assistance. For eight years, in *Splendeurs et misères des courtisanes,* Lucien will lead a glittering but puppet-like existence in the capital which had so recently disowned him. Such will be the false face of Lucien; the true face will be seen when eventually he hangs himself in prison (*I*(6), p. 794). The suicide, which by chance he avoids at the end of *Les Souffrances de l'inventeur,* is (it seems) the ineluctable necessity of his life, stemming from the deepest promptings of his character.

Herrera, to a far greater extent than Lousteau or even Daniel d'Arthez, is the mentor who tries to instruct his protégé in the hidden truths about the world. He is the seer who can use his deep and unclouded vision of the 'real' Paris in order to relaunch Lucien on life and a sort of career, and also to point out to him the various catastrophic mistakes he had made during his thirteen months in the capital. Lucien had not appreciated the inner necessities of Parisian life, although he had come to terms with the external necessities such as the need to wear smart clothes. He had ignored the supreme necessity of concealment, the fourth of the premisses upon which *Illusions perdues* is constructed. He had not realized that, in order to succeed in worldly Parisian life, it was necessary for him not to change political parties but (overtly, at least) to change women (595). Not that he need have abandoned Coralie for Mme de Bargeton altogether. Concealment, or hypocrisy, would — as Herrera suggests — have enabled him to maintain his attachments to both. The only necessity, disregarded by him, was that he should have obtained Mme de Bargeton's talismanic protection by cultivating rather than despising her love. This is the fundamental necessity compared with which such objectives as the official acquisition of a change of surname are

frankly superfluous. Instead, when Mme de Bargeton had beck-
oned him back to her, he had rebuffed her overtures: largely,
perhaps, out of love for Coralie (387) but also, it seems, out of
that hatred which is the other face of sexual love.

Throughout *Illusions perdues,* and indeed the *Comédie
humaine* as a whole, Balzac emphasizes the two faces of reality.
'Tout est bilatéral dans le domaine de la pensée', says Blondet
(360), voicing the fifth and most basic premiss of *Illusions
perdues:* a premiss never more clearly expressed in fictional
terms than in the *Comédie humaine,* and close to the teaching
of Spinoza of whose thought it may be a reflection. 'Les idées
sont binaires. Janus est le mythe de la critique et le symbole
du génie'. Everything — not only literary criticism — has its
two aspects: history, law, chance, and the characters of Lousteau, Mme de Bargeton, Coralie, David Séchard, Lucien above
all! Even the love of Ève and Mme Chardon for Lucien has
its negative aspect, in that it has nurtured his egoism (544).
Where there are not two faces, there are a face and a mask.
Actresses wear a mask in their professional lives, and often,
like Florine, in their private lives also. Diplomats and politi-
cians, like Du Châtelet, Des Lupeaulx and even the Duc de
Rhétoré, wear a mask; as do the journalists who write their
articles under the disguises of a pseudonym or false initials.
The world of journalism is the true sin against the Holy Ghost.
Hence Balzac's assertion (a play of words inspired by Voltaire,
and again put into Blondet's mouth) that 'aussi ... si la Presse
n'existait point, faudrait-il ne pas l'inventer' (309). It is blasphemous, sacrilegious, and more morally pernicious than the
worst doctrines of the Jesuits (379), whose probabilism (indirectly alluded to both by Lousteau and the narrator: 341,
375) similarly emphasizes the two faces of things.

The theatres, like the newspaper offices, are the meeting-
places of masks. In the theatres these masks come together
both on stage and in the foyers. For Lucien, however, the
theatre is a place of magical, dreamlike fascination. The words
'enchantement' and 'magie' are often used by Balzac in connection with the theatre. But the apparently gratuitous magic of
the theatre is an illusion. No world is more subject to the
rigours of illusionism and mechanical contrivance. No world

except journalism is more deceitful and hard-hearted. Elsewhere in *Illusions perdues,* as in the scene of David's sudden appearance out of his hiding-place, Balzac uses the words 'enchantement' (565) or 'magie' (616). Also in Angoulême, not long before David's arrest, Balzac even shows us Cérizet hiding behind some planks whilst David and Petit-Claud walk past on the other side; then speaking to his accomplice in noisy stage whispers, just as if the scene were in a theatre (567). The world is as much of a contrivance as is the theatre (the whole of Balzac's world is the Human *Comedy!*); and it is as subject to inner necessities. Lucien makes the mistake of confusing the tawdry, impotent magic of the theatre with the truly effective magic of the genuine sources of talismanic power.

The 'fiction' which Balzac writes as *Illusions perdues* is not a mask concealing the truth of the 'real' world which it purports to describe. The two faces of the understanding of human events — history and fiction — are interposed as Balzac reminds us of the *fictional* Official History and of the *truthful* Secret History of which his own novel is one example. His novel, a fiction, will reveal the truth about certain aspects of the world. This truth is that certain things within the historical world are a complex fiction in themselves, designed to cheat the unsuspecting and the unsophisticated. The bills piled up by the protesting of the promissory notes in *Les Souffrances de l'inventeur* are not only a device whereby the law produces a manifest injustice; they are also a fictional script written by the lawyers, a game played between them. In the same ludic spirit Balzac plays with the pun *compte/conte;* yet beneath the playfulness is the earnest message that such accounts are fictional. The commercial instrument known as the return account ('ce charmant compte': 493) merits the wittiest condemnation: 'le *Compte de Retour* est un conte plein de fictions terribles' (495); 'jamais les romanciers n'ont inventé de conte plus invraisemblable que celui-là' (491). Balzac's fiction, therefore, is true to the inner realities of life. In an amazing somersault of perception the 'fictional' is suddenly viewed as being essentially true to life, whilst historical reality is full of fictions.

Thus Balzac shows the reader the 'truth' about the world just as Lucien is also shown it. Yet Lucien does not overcome

all his illusions, although his mother and sister do eventually
lose all theirs concerning him (495). The narrative is punctuated
with references to the fact that he still retains illusions (285,
344, 512). Even at the end of *Les Souffrances de l'inventeur* he
may still perhaps entertain illusions concerning his own genius.
He is undoubtedly naïve at his meeting with Herrera. Far from
penetrating to a closer understanding of reality, he seems at
times, towards the end of the novel, to have lost contact with
it altogether: 'Je suis héroïque' (541), 'je suis né prince' (581).
He never discovers, nor are we shown him wondering, why
David came out of hiding and was arrested (580), nor who
had forged the letter which brought David out of his concealment. The reader, therefore, is *shown* much more of the truth
than is divulged to Lucien. And perhaps, on such universal
subjects as the secret meaning of history, the ambivalence of
the law, the egoism of human nature, but not necessarily the
nature of the poetic character, the reader sheds many more
illusions than does Lucien himself!

The theme of triumph is an important one in *Illusions
perdues*, and especially in relation to Lucien who envisages
his career in terms of social triumph (196, 199, 432) and the
intellectual domination (256) of which Balzac himself dreamt
(*4*(1), p. 74), not in D'Arthez's terms of the achievement of
intellectual excellence. And because it reveals to us far more
about Lucien's worldly struggles than about the nature and the
difficulties of poetic writing, *Illusions perdues* is a revelation
of the secret workings of the world, rather than a *Bildungsroman* illuminating the development of character. We do not
witness the young man's struggles with intractable literary
material, nor the complex moral and spiritual torments through
which, in similar circumstances, most sensitive souls would
have gone. Paris is a dehumanizing experience. Lucien himself
resents the fact that it does not treat him like a man (198). The
labyrinthine struggles in which it involves him affect David's
struggles in *Les Souffrances de l'inventeur:* the valiant scientific
efforts are undermined by the self-repudiating forgeries of a
man who is spiritually dead. In the carefully constructed plot
of *Illusions perdues* the role of coincidence is great, and many
of the deeper meanings of the action are only to be teased

out of the actual events. Such is the delicately balanced mechanism whereby, in *Les Souffrances de l'inventeur*, David's arrest and the capturing of his secrets turn on Cérizet's relationship with Henriette Signol. A much deeper irony lies in the dénouement of *Un Grand Homme de province à Paris*, where Lucien writes a hostile review (428) of a *Royalist* book (427), to save his mistress's play which then *fails* (429), only to be challenged to a duel (436-437) for reviews he has *not* written (431), when the only review of D'Arthez's book which he did write was actually *rewritten* by D'Arthez himself (429): here, the deep inner necessities of callous egoism are overlaid with many surface impressions of inconsequentiality. But the deepest irony of all, in that it stems from the central ambiguity, is whether Lucien and Mme de Bargeton are even in love with each other. 'Mme de Bargeton ressentait alors de l'amour pour Lucien', we read on page 387. Yet on the very next page it is implied that this love too was an illusion.

Bibliography

For a better understanding of *Illusions perdues* you should consult some or all of the following books, editions and articles. The more relevant critical works are marked with an asterisk.

OTHER WRITINGS BY BALZAC

1. The new Bibliothèque de la Pléiade edition of the *Comédie humaine* is referred to in any quotation from the *Avant-propos* or novels other than *Illusions perdues*. This edition, published by Gallimard, will consist of twelve volumes, eleven of which have so far appeared (1976-1980).
2. *Le Père Goriot,* University of London Press, 1967.
3. *Splendeurs et misères des courtisanes,* Paris: Gallimard, Coll. Folio, 1973.
4. *Lettres à Madame Hanska,* 4 vols, Paris: Editions du Delta, 1967-71.

OTHER EDITIONS OF 'ILLUSIONS PERDUES'

*5. By Roland Chollet in the new Bibliothèque de la Pléiade edition of the *Comédie humaine,* vol. V, Paris: Gallimard, 1977.
*6. By Jean-Claude Lieber, Paris: Presses de la Renaissance, Coll. L'Univers des livres, 1976.
7. By Antoine Adam, Paris: Garnier, Coll. Classiques Garnier, 1961.

GENERAL WORKS ON BALZAC

*8. Affron, Charles, *Patterns of Failure in 'La Comédie humaine',* Yale U.P., 1966.
9. Alain, *Avec Balzac,* Paris: Gallimard, 1937.
*10. Barbéris, Pierre, *Mythes balzaciens,* Paris: Colin, 1972.
*11. Barbéris, Pierre, *Le Monde de Balzac,* Paris: Arthaud, 1973.
12. Bardèche, Maurice, *Une Lecture de Balzac,* Paris: Les Sept Couleurs, 1964.
*13. Besser, Gretchen R., *Balzac's Concept of Genius. The Theme of Superiority in the 'Comédie humaine',* Geneva: Droz, 1969.
14. Donnard, Jean-Hervé, *Balzac. Les Réalités économiques et sociales dans la 'Comédie humaine',* Paris: Colin, 1961.
*15. Fortassier, Rose, *Les Mondains de 'la Comédie humaine': étude historique et psychologique,* Paris: Klincksieck, 1974.

16. Frappier-Mazur, Lucienne, *L'Expression métaphorique dans la 'Comédie humaine': domaine social et physiologique*, Paris: Klincksieck, 1976.
17. Gauthier, Henri, *L'Homme intérieur dans la vision de Balzac*, 2 vols, Lille: Université de Lille III, 1973.
18. Hunt, Herbert James, *Balzac's 'Comédie humaine'*, London: Athlone Press, 2nd (revised) edn, 1964.
19. Jacques, Georges, *Paysages et structures dans 'la Comédie humaine'*, Louvain: Publications Universitaires de Louvain, 1976.
20. Maurois, André, *Prométhée, ou la Vie de Balzac*, Paris: Hachette, 1965.
*21. Nykrog, Per, *La Pensée de Balzac dans la 'Comédie humaine'. Esquisse de quelques concepts-clé*, Copenhagen: Munksgaard, 1965.
*22. Prendergast, Christopher, *Balzac. Fiction and Melodrama*, London: Arnold, 1978.
23. Preston, Ethel, *Recherches sur la technique de Balzac. Le Retour systématique des personnages dans 'la Comédie humaine'*, Paris: Presses Universitaires, 1926.
*24. Pugh, Anthony R., *Balzac's Recurring Characters*, London: Duckworth, 1975.
*25. Schilling, Bernard N., *The Hero as Failure. Balzac and the Rubempré Cycle*, Chicago U.P., 1968.

SPECIFIC WORK ON 'ILLUSIONS PERDUES'

26. Bérard, Suzanne-Jean, *La Genèse d'un roman de Balzac: 'Illusions perdues'*, 2 vols, Paris: Colin, 1961.

ARTICLES CONCERNING 'ILLUSIONS PERDUES'

27. Citron, Pierre, 'Situations balzaciennes avant Balzac', *L'Année balzacienne*, 1960, pp. 149-160.
28. Clark, Roger, 'Autour d'*Illusions perdues: L'Alcade dans l'embarras'*, *L'Année balzacienne*, 1977, pp. 281-283.
29. Conner, Wayne, 'Sur quelques personnages d'*Un Grand Homme de province à Paris'*, *L'Année balzacienne*, 1961, pp. 185-189.
*30. Gaulmier, Jean, 'Monde balzacien et monde réel: notes sur *Illusions perdues'*, *Balzac and the Nineteenth Century. Studies in French Literature presented to Herbert J. Hunt*, Leicester U.P., 1972, pp. 79-84.
*31. Hunt, Herbert James, 'Balzac's Pressmen', *French Studies*, July 1957, pp. 230-245.
*32. Kanes, Martin, '*Illusions perdues* and the Word Game', *Balzac's Comedy of Words*, Princeton U.P., 1975, pp. 219-259.
*33. Lacaux, André, 'Le Premier Etat d'*Un Grand Homme de province à Paris'*, *L'Année balzacienne*, 1969, pp. 187-210.

34. Lotte, Fernand, 'Le *Retour des personnages* dans *la Comédie humaine*. Avantages et inconvénients du procédé', *L'Année balzacienne*, 1961, pp. 227-281.

*35. Lukács, György, '*Illusions perdues*', *Balzac et le réalisme français*, Paris: Maspéro, 1967, pp. 48-68.

36. Meininger, Anne-Marie, '*Illusions perdues* et faits retrouvés', *L'Année balzacienne*, 1979, pp. 47-75.

*37. Mount, A. J., 'H. de Balzac: *Lost Illusions* (1837-43)', *The Monster in the Mirror: Studies in Nineteenth-Century Realism* (ed. D. A. Williams), Oxford U.P. for University of Hull, 1978, pp. 17-39.

38. Sagnes, Guy, 'Au dossier d'*Illusions perdues*', *L'Année balzacienne*, 1967, pp. 352-355.

*39. Tolley, Bruce R., 'The Cénacle of Balzac's *Illusions perdues*', *French Studies*, 1961, pp. 324-337.

40. Tolley, Bruce R., 'Balzac et les saint-simoniens', *L'Année balzacienne*, 1966, pp. 49-66.